REDISCOVERING NATSUME SŌSEKI

Sōseki in 1908

REDISCOVERING
NATSUME SŌSEKI

WITH THE FIRST ENGLISH TRANSLATION OF
TRAVELS IN MANCHURIA AND KOREA

CELEBRATING THE CENTENARY OF SŌSEKI'S ARRIVAL
IN ENGLAND 1900–1902

INTRODUCTION AND TRANSLATION BY
INGER SIGRUN BRODEY
AND
SAMMY I. TSUNEMATSU

GLOBAL ORIENTAL

Rediscovering Natsume Sōseki
With the first English translation of *Travels in Manchuria and Korea*

Introduction and translation by Inger Sigrun Brodey and Sammy I. Tsunematsu

First published 2000 by
GLOBAL ORIENTAL
PO Box 219
Folkestone
Kent CT20 3LZ

Global Oriental is an imprint of Global Books Ltd

© 2000 GLOBAL BOOKS LTD

ISBN 1-901903-30-3

British Library Cataloguing in Publication Data
A CIP catalogue entry for this book is available
from the British Library

Set in Bembo 11pt by LaserScript, Mitcham, Surrey
Printed and bound in England by Bookcraft Ltd., Midsomer Norton, Avon

Contents

List of Plates

NOTE: Plates 14–22 taken from *Manchuria: A Survey* by Adachi Kinnosuke, New York, Robert M. McBride & Co, 1925.

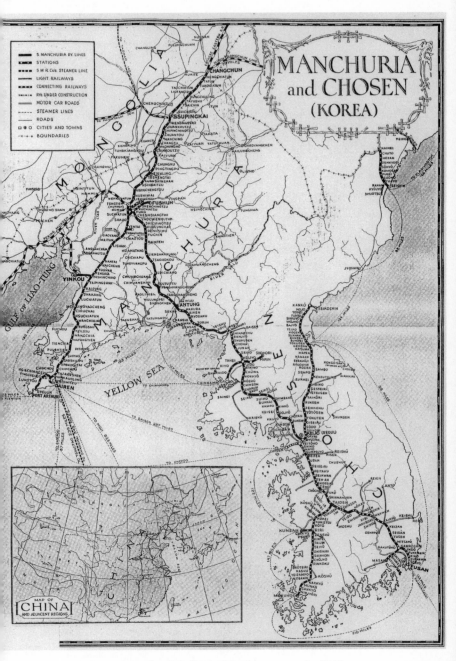

Map of South Manchurian Railway route in 1920s

Introduction

by INGER SIGRUN BRODEY

1 : REDISCOVERING NATSUME SŌSEKI

To a contemporary Japanese audience, the idea of rediscovering Natsume Sōseki could seem preposterous. The man whose face adorns the ¥1000 note and whose novels are still mandatory reading for school children does not appear to need rediscovery in Japan. Hundreds of articles, essays, and monographs on Sōseki[1] are published annually. Sōseki is still known fondly by his pen name, and is widely considered the foremost novelist of the Meiji period (1868–1914), if not in all of modern Japan. In 1907, when he wrote *The Poppy* (*Gubijinsō*), his first novel serialized in the *Asahi* newspaper, department stores produced commemorative *yukata*[2] and rings decorated with poppies. His novels have never ceased to have similar commercial appeal. Recently, another Japanese department store issued expensive replicas of his first blockbuster hits, *I am a Cat* (*Wagahai wa neko de aru*, 1905) and *Botchan* (1906). In short, eighty years after his death, there is still a 'Sōseki buumu' in Japan.

To English-speaking audiences, however, the name Sōseki meets with blank looks – unlike the more familiar names of Mishima, Ōe, and even Kawabata, whose novels have gained greater recognition in the West. It is therefore in the English-speaking West that Sōseki needs not rediscovery, but *discovery*.[3] This discrepancy in Sōseki's popularity is difficult to account for, given the number of his works that have been translated into English, notably Edwin McClellan's excellent translation of *Kokoro*, Sōseki's most famous novel. It is one of our hopes that this edition will help put Sōseki's contributions into a fresh context for Western audiences. Sōseki would seem to have the makings of great popularity in the United States, given the formative influence of East-West relations on his own life and works. In particular, Sōseki's travels to London and his intimate acquaintance with eighteenth-century British literature had a significant effect upon his own understanding of the nature and aims of Japanese literature.

Each of his works reflects, in a different way, Sōseki's struggle with finding the best way for Japan to react to the sudden predominance of Western influence in the modern age. As we will see, this is even the case with his travelogue of Manchuria and Korea, translated into English for the first time in this volume. In his account of Manchuria and the rapid economic and cultural changes that Japan was bringing about via its South Manchurian Railway Company, issues of 'modernization' or 'Westernization' are ubiquitous. In the historical context that Sōseki records here, it is ironically Japan that is attempting to 'Westernize' China, for its own political and cultural reasons.

Part of the significance of *Travels in Manchuria and Korea* is historical. Sōseki was the first major Japanese literary figure to visit Manchuria (or even China) in the modern age, and he visited Manchuria at a particularly interesting historical moment, when the Japanese government was riding high on the waves of its international successes. Having recently defeated its two neighbouring giants, China and Russia (Sino-Japanese War of 1894–5 and the Russo-Japanese War of 1904–5), Japan was just embarking on a grand project of expanding its economic, cultural, and political role in Manchuria through the creation of the South Manchurian Railway Company (SMR). Not only does Sōseki ride the SMR to the inner regions of Manchuria, but he also observes the company's research activities, organizational structure and inner workings. Although Sōseki's descriptions are disappointing to those who would like further political engagement on the author's part regarding the darker sides of SMR activity, Sōseki's more detached descriptions have a cultural significance of their own. They allow Sōseki to use his literary techniques, imagery, and symbolism to indicate the delicate position of the Meiji government, and the complicated Meiji response to its position in international affairs.

Too often, however, the historical significance of *Travels in Manchuria and Korea* has blinded readers to its literary significance. *Travels* also helps us better understand the place of Manchuria in Sōseki's literary imagination. Within the pages of *Travels*, we find discussion that illuminates his other writings. The reader of *Kofu* (or *The Miner*) will be intrigued by his description of mining in Manchuria; his treatment of Western-style consumption and postwar exuberance carries over from *Sore kara* (*And Then*); and his use of colour symbolism is almost as vibrant as it is in *Sanshiro*.

The fact that Manchuria reappears in his later novels *Mon* and *Higan Sugi Made* suggests its significance for him as symbol, both as a frontier for new opportunity, as well as a symbol of exile. And as

Sōseki visits the Bay of Port Arthur, where General Nogi suffered his embarrassing losses during the Russo-Japanese War, the reader will remember the same general who indirectly causes Sensei's death in *Kokoro*. A travel narrative is itself a natural way of encountering Sōseki, whether for the first time or as a rediscovery, for Sōseki is, as we will see below, a born traveller. In *Travels*, Sōseki develops a narrative technique that itself conveys his idiosyncratic stance towards his surroundings, in some ways reminiscent of Laurence Sterne's sentimental traveller.[4] Almost all Sōseki's central heroes travel, for travel not only lies at the heart of Meiji experience, but it also defines Sōseki as an individual.

□

Meiji Intellect, Meiji Solitude

We will first consider some of the reasons for Sōseki's popularity in Japan, where Sōseki is considered the Meiji intellectual *par excellence*. His own inner struggles and turmoil over issues of abandonment and alienation, visible just beneath the surface of all his literature, have become synonymous with an entire era; people read Sōseki in order to understand Japan at this crucial moment of confrontation with the West and with modernization. (In the Meiji era there was little, if any, distinction made between modernization and Westernization.) Since Japan continues to struggle with its identity *vis-à-vis* the West, Sōseki's popularity would suggest that he still provides fresh insight into these matters. In particular, Sōseki's profound sense of what is lost to Japan in its processes of modernization strikes resonance even today.

Sōseki also had the additional quality of combining two traits, each worthy of respect, and seldom combined in one individual: namely, he was both a respected scholar, of Chinese as well as of British literature, and yet also unpretentious. Although his command of English was astonishingly good and his ability to compose poems in Chinese style (*kanshi*) unequalled in modern Japan,[5] he nonetheless maintained his identity as Japanese, and he took the sensational step of leaving a high academic post in favour of writing for the general public. In the process, he somewhat disdainfully rejected Japan's highest academic awards to live the life of a novelist. Almost all his popular novels and other writings appeared in serial form in the *Asahi* newspaper. As Norma Field has remarked, Sōseki differed from other masters of Japanese modern literature in that he was a popular writer who 'touched upon popular concerns in an accessible manner' (Field, 277). This powerful combination of the respectability of a Tokyo Imperial

3

University professor, a pronounced sense of humour, and an accessible manner, may underlie his continued popularity with university students and general readers alike in Japan today.

Since he is regarded as representative of his era, Sōseki's popularity is also closely connected with the details of his life, which coincided almost exactly with the long reign of Emperor Meiji (1868–1912), and thus with the Meiji Era that witnessed unprecedented change in Japan. He was born in 1867, in Edo, one year before it was renamed Tokyo (becoming the new seat of the emperor) and fourteen years after Admiral Perry's first visit to Japan, an arrival that heralded the official, forced opening of Japanese ports to Western trade. In 1868, Emperor Meiji announced his 'Five Point Plan' (or 'Five Articles') that ousted the samurai from their seats of power, allowed freedom of belief and of occupation in Japan, and promoted Western-style education in order to promote 'civilization'. The following decades witnessed a fascination (or 'intoxication', as it was called) with things Western, leading to sights that would have been unimaginable only a decade earlier. Traditional woodblock prints[6] and photographs document such sights as an Emperor who wore Western suits and cut off his topknot, and Japanese dignitaries learning to waltz, play the violin, and eat with knives and forks (see Plate 13). Alongside these cultural changes occurred the technological and industrial advances that transformed the Japanese economy and urban landscapes. Sōseki lived to see the death of Emperor Meiji in 1912, and died four years later, in 1916.

From the beginning, Sōseki's life was characterized by continuing crises over his sense of belonging, partly as a result of the cultural upheaval taking place around him. The sad events of the first ten years of his life seem to have been particularly formative, as Doi Takeo has argued in his psychoanalytical study of Sōseki. These events – which led to a powerful sense of dislocation – are also particularly interesting in coming to understand his popular image as representative of the Meiji Era. Sōseki's parents were upper-class administrators (*nanushi*) of the local samurai, and although not samurai themselves, found their social standing suddenly undercut with the collapse of the feudal system. At the time of Sōseki's birth, his parents were 51 and 42 years old, and already had seven children, including four sons. Their social embarrassment over such a late birth, it is said, added to their financial embarrassments, and, as a result, they gave away Sōseki to a local greengrocer. The greengrocer and his family, busy with their daily work, neglected Sōseki, leaving him outside their shop in a basket, where his crying would not disturb them. Finally, taking pity upon her young brother lying outside in the cold, one of Sōseki's sisters brought him home to his natural parents. His parents tolerated his presence for a year or so until they gave him away again, this time to a childless former servant and his wife. Domestic troubles and indiscretions committed by this second adoptive father caused his new mother twice to seek protection at Sōseki's family house, and eventually led to the divorce of the couple as well as to Sōseki's final return to his original family. Even when Sōseki returned home to his mother and father for the final time, he thought they were more distant relatives. In a memorable episode, it was not until a kindly nursemaid whispered the secret to him in the dark of night that he knew he had returned to his natural parents. His three successive families, the two aborted attempts to give him away, and his three name changes all lent considerable chaos to Sōseki's first years of life.

Just as Sōseki travelled as a young child and grew to be a stranger in his own home, not even recognizing his own parents, Sōseki describes the modern Meiji man as straddling cultures, dislocated both from Japan's past as well as from its future. This modern man, as Sōseki depicts him, is divorced from the innocence and moral integrity connected with Japan's neo-Confucian past, and at the same time is inexorably attracted to modernity, the West, material success, and conspicuous consumption. It is not just the case that Sōseki's life is interpreted retrospectively as symbolic of the Meiji era; Sōseki himself 'saw his own difficulties as symbolic of the historical predicament of his nation' (Hibbet, 317). His heroes are all victims of an age of change, and help him depict the alienation of the modern intellectual from native certainty, as well as the corruption and isolation that inherently accompany cultural sophistication. As a character says in his novel *Kokoro*: 'You see, loneliness is the price we have to pay for being born in this modern age, so full of freedom, independence, and our own egotistical selves!' In Etō Jun's words, Sōseki never tired of describing 'the spiritual half-death of modern man' (Etō, 612): Sōseki's literature continues to dwell on the themes of the inescapable loneliness and individualism of the modern world, and to provide insight into the development of Japanese culture.

□

Sōseki's Intellectual Travels Westwards

In his autobiographical account *Recollections* (*Omoidasu kotonado*, 82), Sōseki reports that he once half-jokingly consulted a priest about his future. The priest's response was a curious mixture of prediction and advice that Sōseki conveys with his usual sense of humour: 'You will go west and still further west,' predicted the priest. Then, after studying Sōseki's face, he added: 'You should grow a beard and buy a house quickly.' When Sōseki wondered about the connection between the beard and the house, the priest's response was curiously aesthetic. He complained about the asymmetry caused by the moustache that divided Sōseki's face in half; a beard, he said, would help him 'gain composure'. This image is interesting from a Meiji perspective, since moustaches were symbolic of the West. A beard, therefore, was not only a token of 'settling down', but also suggested a kind of nationalism. Whereas Sōseki seems to have found the comment about the beard a curious digression from the prediction of his travels westwards, the first comment could easily be interpreted as the priest's reaction to Sōseki's moustache, perhaps even as an antidote to the effects of his anticipated Westernization. In fact, the priest was right: Sōseki did travel gradually westwards both geographically and intellectually. In *Recollections*, he jokingly blames the fact that he neither settled down nor bought a house on the fact that he had never adequately followed the priest's aesthetic advice.

Intellectually, Sōseki also migrated westwards, from Japanese literature, to English language studies, and finally to English literature, in the space of a decade. In middle school, the young Meiji school system offered two tracks – in addition to the regular track, there was an accelerated track that emphasized English and Western learning for those who would succeed in the modern world. Sōseki objected to this division of education, and chose the traditional route, falling in love with traditional Chinese poetry. Sōseki 'despised the English language and rejected the view that the study of English would translate into financial success' (Gessel, 18). At the time, he considered a career as a writer of Japanese literature, but was dissuaded by his brother who told him that writing was by no means a 'profession' – that is, in a neo-Confucian sense, an occupation that would benefit the nation as well as oneself. Sōseki seems to have been persuaded by his brother, because by 1883, when he had completed middle school, he enrolled in a preparatory school to improve his knowledge of English, before proceeding to college.

By the time he entered the College of Tokyo Imperial University, his goal was to become a Japanese-style architect. Again, he was persuaded by a friend to do otherwise. 'How can Japan, an impoverished nation, compete with the great and wealthy countries of the West? A Japanese architect could never hope to build anything that would rival a timeless edifice like St

Paul's', his friend objected. His eventual choice of entering the English Department at Tokyo Imperial University, Japan's most prestigious university, rather than studying Chinese literature, bears some consideration. Scholars tend to see it as Sōseki's final, characteristically ambivalent, acquiescence to the inevitable forces of modernization. Etō Jun writes that the 'decision to embrace English literature no doubt reflected Sōseki's fears of being left behind by the future'.[7] Thus, the modern situation impelled Sōseki to study what he disliked. He nevertheless excelled in his studies, and in 1893, received the second bachelor's degree awarded in Japan for studies in English literature.

Within the pages of *Travels in Manchuria and Korea*, Sōseki frequently records flashbacks of his school days, particularly his days at the preparatory school, where he was endeavouring to improve his English in order to gain entrance to college. It was at the preparatory school that he met his primary travel guide on the journey, Nakamura Zekō, president of the powerful South Manchurian Railway Company that conveys Sōseki from location to location. In the course of his travels, he meets several friends from his school days, and indulges in flashbacks of their schemes, laziness, and failing grades. He portrays his classmates, along with himself, as students who competed to get the worst grades in the class and who spent their time demolishing their living quarters with miniature cannonballs and riotous antics. Here, the fictional character of *Travels in Manchuria and Korea* becomes overt in the separation between the narrator and the historical Sōseki. In *Travels*, Sōseki does not portray his conversion to serious studies, when he made his 'solemn vow' to succeed. It was a vow he kept, remaining at the top of his class until graduation. We will consider below why Sōseki might wish to disguise aspects of his own character and to create a less goal-driven narrator in this work. We will also return to why it might be significant that so much of his Manchurian travelogue deals with the remote past – particularly his initial failure to learn English during his schooldays in Japan.

□

Official Travel to England

Geographically, Sōseki's travels westwards took him first from his stable teaching positions in Tokyo to inferior positions in the hinterland of Japan – first to Matsuyama, then Kumamoto on the southern island of Kyūshu. From there, he headed off to London, by governmental decree, to become Japan's first Japanese English literary scholar to go to England and study English Literature.

Sōseki chose to attend University College, London, rather than Cambridge, Oxford, or Edinburgh, the other options he considered. While he was disgusted by what he saw as the low level of competence among the students at the University College, he chose it over the other universities for three reasons. First, he despised the élitism of Oxford and Cambridge. Second, smacking slightly of sour grapes, he complained that he would never be able to become a Cambridge 'gentleman' because of his small government stipend. He later wrote:

> I was inclined to go to either Oxford or Cambridge, since they were centres of learning well-known even to us. ... I took the opportunity of going [to Cambridge] to see what sort of place it was ... I met two or three Japanese there. They were all sons and younger brothers of wealthy merchants, who were prepared to spend thousands of yen per year in order to become 'gentlemen'. My allowance from the government was ¥1800 a year. In a place where money controlled everything, I could hardly hope to compete with those people ... I thought ... I do not know if the gentlemen of England are so impressive as to make it worth my while to imitate them; besides, having already spent my youth in the Orient, why should I now start learning how to conduct myself from these English gentlemen who are younger than I am? (McClellan, *Two*, 11).

A third reason for choosing London was that Sōseki assumed that the best and most 'authentic' English accents must be found in the capital city. In London, he studied privately with W.J.Craig, editor of the *Arden Shakespeare*, avoided contact with Englishmen as much as possible, and immersed himself in reading, purchasing, and studying eighteenth-century literature. He also read a wide range of complementary books in other disciplines that he thought would help him in his ambitious goal of understanding and defining the essential differences between Western and Japanese literature.

The two-year trip to England nearly drove Sōseki to a nervous breakdown. In *Tower of London* (*London no Tō*, 1907), he writes: 'The two years I spent in London were the most unpleasant two years of my life. Among English gentlemen, I lived like a shaggy dog in a pack of wolves' (*Zenshu* XI:10, IX: 14). On the one hand, such remarks seem to convey his antipathy for the English; yet there are other strikingly self-deprecatory passages that suggest that he felt inferior to the Englishmen around him, particularly with regard to appearance:

Everyone I see on the street is tall and good-looking. That, first of all, intimidates me, embarrasses me. Sometimes I see an unusually short man, but he is still two inches taller than I am, as I compare his height with mine as we pass each other. Then I see a dwarf coming, a man with an unpleasant complexion–and it turns out to be my own reflection in the shop window (*Zenshu,* XII: 36–37).

Sōseki's letters from this period are full of bitterness over his impoverished position in England, since the governmental allowance was inadequate to his needs. This personal impoverishment was exacerbated by Sōseki's twin desires – both to represent Japanese civilization with honour and also to adapt to the English lifestyle. He was ashamed of the figure he cut in England, partly because he did not want Japan to be thought an 'impoverished and backward' nation, or worse yet, a 'dwarf'.

One particularly interesting story that Sōseki recounts in *Tower of London* of his stay in England makes a curious reappearance in the pages of *Travels*. During his stay in London, Sōseki's Japanese sense of decorum occasioned him to feel that he was unable to partake in any evening activities without a Western-style evening suit. After much worry over the price of such a suit, he found a cheap tailor on Tottenham Court Road, and had one made. In his letters home, he complains a great deal about his impoverishment and justifies this expense at great length. In *Tower of London*, the suit becomes a symbol of Sōseki's sense of incomplete assimilation into England, his makeshift appearance as a foreigner, and the unpolished figure that he thought he presented. It also testifies to his sense of inauthenticity, posing as a Westerner in 'borrowed clothes'.

Interestingly, the story of the evening suit reappears in the account of his travels to Manchuria, his other major trip to a foreign country. In *Travels*, it reappears in the context of once again struggling to find something appropriate to wear to a Western-style evening event – a 'ball'. In this scene from Chapter 7, we see Sōseki gloating over his international savvy, his knowledge of what one wears to an evening party, as opposed to his more rustic friend Nakamura Zekō, the President of the SMR (see Plate 1). Sōseki laughs at his friend's idea of going in formal Japanese garb, suggesting that Japanese dress would look ridiculous at a ball, and utterly disqualify them from doing what one should at a ball – namely, dance. Yet, even in Manchuria, Sōseki still portrays himself as struggling to fit into Western ways of life and dress. And in both cases, it is clear that Sōseki sees himself as a representative of Japan, and as a symbol of the Japanese presence and potential abroad.

The stay in London greatly intensified Sōseki's sense of alienation and his life-long preoccupation with physical appearances and ailments. Despite his advanced mastery of English language and literature, Sōseki was increasingly oppressed by a sense of inability to master the language fully – a sense of inadequacy that explicitly plagues the narrator of *Travels* as well. His lofty ambitions, therefore, along with an intense self-consciousness led him to becoming markedly defensive in his social circles; it also engendered severe bouts of depression. Among the Japanese community in London, he was rumoured to have gone insane.

□

Manchuria and the West

Sōseki's trip to London was probably the most formative experience in his entire life. It is this experience that contemporary readers talk about when they discuss Sōseki's travels abroad. Sōseki's other major overseas trip – the one to Manchuria and Korea recounted in this volume – should be understood in this context.[8] Seven years after his return from England, Sōseki must have been struck by the reversal of his situation. On the second trip, he was wined and dined in first-class, Western-style accommodation all the way from Tokyo to central Manchuria and on to the Korean peninsula. In fact, all the luxuries of the South Manchurian Railway, and its guides, vehicles, hotels, and food, were provided to him free of charge. Rather than feeling ashamed of the impoverished figure he cut as a Japanese representative in London, Sōseki could now glory in the modern accommodation and economic prowess displayed by the Japanese in Manchuria. The reader of *Travels*, therefore, will note the frequent, explicit comparisons that Sōseki makes with Japan and the West. Consider, for example, his descriptions of carriages and of architecture in the Manchurian city of Dairen (the Japanese name for Talien): the elegant carriages in which he rides are so resplendent that 'even in the very heart of Tokyo, one could not easily have found their like' (Chapter 4). Then again, when he sees an imposing bridge in Port Arthur, it was 'so elegant and robust' that one 'could really have imagined oneself in the heart of Europe' (Chapter 7). In the Manchurian manifestations of modernization, the Japanese are continually compared with Europeans and the West. Interestingly, this latter bridge bears the name 'Nihonbashi' or 'Bridge of Japan', which was the bridge in Edo from which all distances were measured, making it even more symbolic of Japanese national pride. In fact, when Sōseki's love of architecture reveals itself in the frequent descriptions of architecture that are scattered through the pages of *Travels*, it is interesting to note that the architecture he describes is almost exclusively either Western-style, Japanese, or an awkward combination of the two. Chinese or Manchurian architecture is curiously, somewhat conspicuously, absent.

Throughout the pages of *Travels*, Sōseki makes frequent references to Western things, particularly as he starts his account of the departure from Shimonoseki and the boat ride to Dairen, when his surroundings seem drenched with novelty and exoticism. The people that appear in the narrative, particularly in these opening chapters, are primarily Westerners. Apparently, Japanese would travel for a day out to Yokohama during this period in order to view foreigners; in a sense, Sōseki was appealing to just such excited curiosity in his opening chapters. He spends a good deal of time describing Western noses, choosing to peruse Western magazines, and admiring Western suits. Just as in London, though, he also avoids engaging in conversation with Westerners, even when it pains others, as he describes in the following passage:

> When we had lunch, I felt sorry for the English people who did not use chopsticks or eat rice. It was surprising that the British Consul, who had lived in China for eighteen years, was completely incapable of using chopsticks. On the other hand, he expressed himself remarkably well in Mandarin Chinese. Matsuda, who was very busy, left the table and was unable to return. The man who replaced him as our host had a difficult task, speaking to the British people in English and to us in Japanese. However, neither Hashimoto nor I myself made use of our English. The English, by nature, are stamped with arrogance, and unless they have been introduced, are not very willing to talk to somebody from elsewhere. That is why we showed the same arrogance towards the British people (Chapter 51).

The passage reveals his continuing anxiety about assimilation and his lingering ambivalence about speaking English. There is only one occasion when he actually speaks with a foreigner, presumably in English: this occurs in Chapter 6, when he is forced to sit at a dinner table with an old man who sneezes continually and repeats himself as though he had never spoken with Sōseki at all. The only foreign conversation he portrays, therefore, is remarkably unsuccessful, and characterized by a complete and ludicrous lack of connection.

Despite the Asian destinations in *Travels*, and despite the great reversal in his social status *vis-à-vis* the inhabitants of the countries he visits, there is nonetheless a striking consistency in Sōseki's stance. He consistently emphasizes his social awkwardness, and his position as outsider, even while travelling in Asia. Strangely enough, Manchuria itself often seems absent from the travelogue – lost in the intensity of the comparison between Japan and the West, an omission that is suggestive of the larger historical picture and Meiji Japan's struggles with identity.

II : REDISCOVERING *TRAVELS IN MANCHURIA AND KOREA*

T he remarkable document translated here into English for the first time is a travel narrative of Sōseki's six-week trip through Manchuria and Korea in the autumn of 1909. It has generally ranked as one of the least popular of Sōseki's writings, both in Japan and abroad; it is therefore in need of *rediscovery* in Japan, as well as discovery in English-speaking countries. An interested reader has to thumb through many volumes of biographies and critical works on Sōseki even to find mention of this work. The reasons for its unpopularity are themselves interesting, as we shall see below, and are also symptomatic of the great anxiety aroused in readers, Japanese and English-speaking alike, about the historical events that form the backdrop of *Travels*.

Sōseki departed from Tokyo, and travelled first by steamship and then by the South Manchurian Railway up the Liaodong peninsula, reaching as far north as Fushun (see Plate 15); he then proceeded on the railway through Andong and on to the Korean Peninsula. The travel narrative that he published only traces his itinerary as far as his arrival in Fushun, and stops short of the Fushun coal mines, as well as of Korea. It is unclear exactly why Sōseki undertook this major trip, although there was a mixture of reasons. Clearly influential was the encouragement of his old school friend Nakamura Zekō, who became the second President of the South Manchurian Railway Company (SMR). Zekō (as Sōseki calls him in the narrative) knew what Sōseki's distinguished name could mean as a vehicle for advertising his young railway company. In addition, we know that the Asahi newspaper, which published all Sōseki's fictional works after he left his university position in 1907, sponsored the trip, and that the SMR paid for his lodging, travel, and guides. In the narrative, the only reason Sōseki mentions is the encouragement from his friend Zekō; he seems to distance himself, however, from Zekō's ambition as well as from the publicity goals of the SMR.

□

The Sino-Japanese War and the Russo-Japanese War

In order to capture the significance of *Travels*, it is necessary to consider it within the context of the historical moment that Sōseki records in his idiosyncratic way. Sōseki's trip occurs just four years after Japan's victory over Russia in 1905 (see Plate 12), a victory that was intensified in that it came only ten years after China, too, suffered a humiliating defeat at the hands of the Japanese in 1895. These two victories over such powerful neighbours produced an unequalled exuberance in the Japanese public and attracted worldwide attention. The Japan that so recently had disbanded the samurai system and opened itself to foreign influences defeated not only its old grandfather China, but also Russia – a modern, industrialized, Western nation.[9]

The Japanese relationship with China was quite complex, blending admiration for China's grand cultural history with disdain for its current poverty, political upheavals, and mass confusion. On the one hand, the Japanese people recognized their cultural debt to China and felt the ties of *kanji bunka* (a popular Meiji notion that the written language shared by China and Japan implied deeper understanding between the cultures). On the other hand, Japanese wartime propaganda emphasized that the Sino-Japanese War was 'not a struggle over power or territory, but a conflict between a backward-looking China seeking to keep an equally backward-looking Korea under its control and a progressive, forward-looking Japan determined to bring the benefits of "civilization" to the peninsula' (Duus, Myers, Peattie, xx).[10] In the negotiations over the Shimonoseki Treaty, which ended the Sino-Japanese War, Japan's desire to court the favour of Western nations led it to acquiesce to pressure from the 'Triple Intervention' of France, Germany, and Russia to relinquish one of its principle gains – control over the Liaodong Peninsula. Still, the victory sent ripples of self-confidence through the Japanese nation, although it was not long before Japan regretted conceding the Liaodong Peninsula. From the turn of the century, Japan then began sending large numbers of Japanese to China, as it had into Taiwan and Korea, in order to maintain its political and economic influence in those countries.

The Russians were not entirely disinterested in their desire to prevent a Japanese claim on the Liaodong Peninsula, and steadily built up their presence in China after helping to settle the Sino-Japanese War. When the European powers intervened to limit the advantages derived from Japan's victory over China in 1895, they installed Germans in the Bay of Jiaozhou, French troops in Guangshouwan, and Russians in Liaodong and in Korea. Whereas the other troops gradually withdrew, Russian troops increased in number. In fact, after joining in an international effort to crush the Boxer Rebellion in 1900, the number of Russian troops grew dramatically. The Russo-Japanese War (1904–5) broke out after a period of diplomatic bickering over the Russian build-up in Southeastern Manchuria and neighbouring regions, particularly on the Liaodong Peninsula and the Korean Peninsula. The war thus stemmed from disputes over boundaries between Japanese and Russian spheres of influence in Manchuria, which was still ruled by the very weak Qing emperor, and also from Japanese disappointment over the European pressure on the Shimonoseki treaty.

The war itself was short, extremely bloody, and fought mainly on the Manchurian mainland and in the Bay of Port Arthur. The torpedoing of three Russian ships at Port Arthur by the Japanese on 8 February 1904 marked the outbreak of the war. While the Japanese fleet maintained the blockade, Generals Oku and Nogi besieged General Stoessel's Russian garrison. While there were many battles during this brief war, this is one of the two to which Sōseki draws the reader's attention. During the naval siege at Port Arthur, General Nogi suffered embarrassing losses – 69,000 out of 120,000 troops. The embarrassing failure ultimately helped cause General Nogi's dramatic self-immolation after the death of Emperor Meiji – an event that becomes an important part of the plot of Sōseki's novel *Kokoro*. Later, the Russian squadrons attempted unsuccessfully to break out on 10 April (on the death of Admiral Makarov) and again on 10 August, but the Japanese sailors still managed to maintain their blockade, despite their many casualties. On 15 December, the siege of Hill 203, the hill that had dominated the trade route, forced the squadron to disperse. The Russian garrison then surrendered on 2 January 1905, after a resistance which cost the Japanese more than 50,000 men. The outcome of the war was decided at the 24-hour-long Battle of Tsushima, where the Japanese fleet, led by Admiral Tōgō, severely damaged the Russian fleet, which had been brought from the Baltic.

In travelling along the South Manchurian Railway line, Sōseki is tracing a route of national Japanese glory; however, he does not admit this. He visits two of the bloodiest scenes of the Russo-Japanese War, although in the second case somewhat reluctantly. First he visits Hill 203 and then he visits the Bay of Port Arthur, where the Russian ships were first sunk, and the many Japanese sailors died. The eventual victory over Russia was the Meiji government's proudest international moment and there would have been great interest on the part of Sōseki's readers to hear his account of these sites.

'The Japanese victory was widely taken to signify Japan's coming of age, its right to stand shoulder-to-shoulder with the nations of the West for the first time since the humiliating years of the forced opening' (Field, 270). Sōseki recorded some of this post-war bombast and ostentation in his novel, *Sore kara* (*And Then*), which he wrote immediately before *Travels to Manchuria and Korea* (see Plate 12). Another novel that he wrote in the same year, *Sanshiro*, includes a scene in which the Russo-Japanese War is featured in an interesting way. The youthful hero encounters an unusual, cosmopolitan, yet impoverished man on the train. Turning from the subject of the beauty of Western women as though there were no change of topic, the man says:

> We Japanese are sad-looking things next to them. We can beat the Russians, we can become a first-class power, but it doesn't make any difference. We've still got the same faces, the same feeble little bodies . . . . Oh yes, this is your first trip to Tokyo, isn't it? You've never seen Mount Fuji. We go by it a little farther on. It's the finest thing Japan has to offer, the only thing we've got to boast about. The trouble is, of course, it's just a natural object. It's been sitting there for all time. We didn't make it (*Sanshiro,* 15).

It is interesting that Sōseki chose the moment of international glory to portray this kind of anxiety about Japan's place in the world order. But part of his point, of course, is that these two feelings are very closely intertwined: the sense of glory and ambition was proportionate to the anxiety Japan felt about its international image.

> Sanshiro had never expected to meet anyone like this after the Russo-Japanese War. The man was almost not a Japanese, he felt. . . . Anyone who had dared say such a thing in Kumamoto would have been taken out and thrashed, perhaps even arrested for treason. . . . Sanshiro did not know what to make of him (*Sanshiro,* 15).

Part of the post-war ostentation that Sōseki gently mocks was due to the anxiety caused by the Portsmouth settlement that ended the war. Although Japanese acquisitions were quite substantial, the Japanese government was disappointed by not receiving the reception it had hoped for from the European powers and the United States. Japan thought it had earned more equal status through its victory over Russia.

In the Portsmouth Treaty, Japan received official recognition of its occupation of Korea namely, the transfer from Russia of the southern branch of the Chinese Eastern Railway, and an official lease of the Southern part of the Liaodong Peninsula, called the Gwandun Leasehold. It also gradually acquired the South Manchurian Railway and jurisdiction over the lands alongside the 100-mile stretch of strategic railway. In Chapters 4–49 of *Travels*, Sōseki travels through the southern half of this historic, acquired railway zone. Only one year after Sōseki's travelogue was published, Japan formally annexed Korea in 1910.

□

The South Manchurian Railway

The South Manchurian Railway (*Minami Manshū Tetsudō Kabushiki Kaisha*) ranks as one of the most powerful and interesting institutions in the history of the complex relations between China, Russia, Korea, and Japan. It was much more than its name would suggest: not merely a transportation company, it played a fundamental part in the development of the Japanese political, economic, and cultural presence in the Liaoning region. These expanded roles of the company's activities become very clear to the reader of *Travels*. By the provisions of the Treaty of Portsmouth, signed on 5 September 1905, which put an end to the Russo-Japanese War, Russia ceded to Japan that part of the East China railway line (*Tōzai Tetsudō*) which was situated in Southern Manchuria. Strictly speaking, this was the 'Chang Chun' line, running from Port Arthur to Harbin, a distance of some 752 kilometres, unsurpassed through the important historical and economic centre of Chang Chun, formerly known as Hsin Ching ('The New Capital'). Following further negotiations with the Chinese government, an additional clause was added to the Sino-Japanese Treaty in Peking, in December, 1905. This clause gave Japan the right to control and manage the Chang Chun line, the Fushun and Yen Tai mining concessions, and also the right to reconstruct and manage the 276 kilometres-long Andong line (Mukden-Andong) – a railway originally operated by the army (see map on page vii).

An Imperial decree issued on 7 June 1906 created the Southern Manchurian Railway Company with the statutes of a limited company, and a massive initial capital investment of ¥200 million. Half the funding was contributed by the Japanese imperial government; the other half was divided between the Chinese State and Chinese or Japanese private shareholders by floating a public subscription. On 1 January 1907, the company began its commercial activities. The directors were appointed by the Japanese government itself. To give a sense of the size of the national investment in this operation, 78% of the total funds invested by the Japan Industrial Bank (*Nihon Kōgyo Ginkō*) between 1905 and 1914 went into SMR bonds.

From the start, therefore, the SMR was a curious hybrid of an independent, profit-generating business venture and a political mission with an implicit military agenda. Within *Travels,* Sōseki gives a hint of this odd mix when he is staying at one of the SMR official hotels (all named Yamato, after the homeland). The fancy hotel is located in the middle of a deserted and impoverished ghost town – an oasis of fresh-cut flowers and damask in the midst of semi-occupied and abandoned buildings. Suddenly, when pondering the scene out his window, he realizes or remembers this aspect of the SMR:

> 'There are only ruins over here,' I thought, returning to my room. A snow-white sheet had been unfolded on the bed; a soft carpet covered the floor. A luxurious armchair had been placed in the room. All the furniture was new and flawlessly matched. There was a stark contrast between the interior and the exterior. I was struck by this contradictory feeling, until it occurred to me that this Yamato Hotel, managed by the Manchurian Railway Company, could certainly not be a profit-making venture. Descending to the dining room, I smelled an abundance of flowers outside the windows. (Chapter 22)

The SMR Yamato hotels had other goals than those of most hotels – namely, political goals.[11]

The Railway Zone operated almost like an independent state within Manchuria, with the power to levy taxes, maintain police forces, handle real estate, operate schools, undertake public works, and provide medical services for the inhabitants of the lands adjacent to the railway line. The SMR sought 'through control over Manchuria to gain the same commercial and industrial privileges granted to Western powers elsewhere in China' (Itō, 5). Between 1906 and 1931, the SMR dominated and monopolized the economic life of Manchuria very successfully, through the management of its harbours and water transportation. The SMR also controlled warehousing, coal mines, electric power, real estate, iron works, industrial plants, natural resources, the labour market, and monetary facilities.

The SMR's founder and first president, Gotō Shimpei, was remarkably blunt about the purposes of the railway company. His intention was that the Japanese should strengthen their position in

China for another Russo-Japanese War by turning Manchuria into an occupied colony and building what Peter Duus and others have called the 'informal empire' of Japan.[12] He clearly wanted Manchuria to remain under Japanese control, and proposed the emigration of 500,000 Japanese to the area (Itō, viii). Gotō called the SMR a 'cultural invasion', or 'Military preparedness in civil garb' (bunsō teki bubi). Here is the passage at greater length:

> ... In short, colonial policy is military preparedness in civil garb; it is carting out the hegemon's strategies under the flag of the kingly way. Such a colonial policy is inescapable in our time. What facilities, then, are necessary to see it through?
>
> We have to implement a cultural invasion with a Central Laboratory, popular education for the resident populace, and forge other academic and economic links. Invasion may not be an agreeable expression, but [language] aside we can generally call our policy one of invasion in civil garb ... (Itō, 14).

As these and the other foundational SMR documents convey, there was a close link between the SMR and the Japanese Gwandung army in Manchuria that persisted beyond the founding of the semi-independent SMR in 1906. Sōseki visited the Railway headquarters only two years after it had donned its 'civilian garb'. In the decades following Sōseki's visit, the SMR became increasingly linked to the military agenda of the Japanese government, until the Manchurian Incident, when the civilian 'front' was officially dropped. Once the military had employed direct force in Manchuria, the SMR became an adjunct to the military, and as a result, when the military collapsed in 1945, so did the SMR.

The SMR did, however, undertake some remarkable research and make some notable industrial advances, using Manchuria's vast natural resources. In Travels, Sōseki visits the SMR's Central Laboratory and other sites where he sees experiments with colza oil, soybean production, silk made from moths, electricity plants, and more. In fact, the SMR boasted about having succeeded, not just in bringing Japan to China, but rather in Westernizing China. In SMR's Manchuria, they claimed, one could find 'Occidental civilization transplanted overnight in an Oriental setting' (Manchuria: Land of Opportunities, 7). It is instructive to note the wording in the SMR publications, written to attract foreign investments in 1922. One such example is given below:

> The once 'forbidden Land' has been opened not only to the world at large, but, more particularly, to the Chinese themselves, who

never dreamed that such golden opportunities lay at their very doors. Less than a generation ago the Russians opened up parts of this country, but it has been the Japanese who have made it a land of opportunity for the world (*Manchuria: Land of Opportunities*, 6).

It is generally thought today that, contrary to the claims of the SMR propaganda, the Chinese were not the beneficiaries of this rapid development. The wages of Chinese labourers were kept to a minimum, housing was of the lowest quality; and worker casualties were high. More than 114,000 Chinese were either killed or seriously injured on the job during the period from 1909 to 1931. In *Travels*, Sōseki makes apparent the poverty of the Chinese, their dangerous working environments, and the inferior housing provided by the SMR, as well as expressing appropriate amazement at the SMR's remarkable industrial achievements. It may be that Sōseki's overall impression of the SMR is best summarized by his first impression of the SMR President's official residence (and SMR headquarters) in Dairen, which the narrator visits in Chapter 5:

> I entered the house. Mr Numata preceded me and opened a thick door at the end of the hallway. When I cast a glance through the opening and surveyed the room beyond, I noticed that it was astonishingly vast. Figures are not my forte, but even if I had known the exact number of *tatami* mats it would have taken to fill that room, it still would not have conveyed its majesty. [13] It made me think of a sanctuary in a Buddhist temple, or of an entire building constructed to a great length. ... It was not until later on, listening to the people's explanations, that I learned that this room, which really was too vast for a reception lounge, actually served as a dance hall. ... Having said this, however, I should have felt more at ease had I been informed of this earlier: I would not have been so baffled at being suddenly taken, without warning, into the sanctuary of a temple from which Buddha was absent. During my stay in Dairen, I passed through this hall several times in order to reach Zekō's office. Only once, on the first visit, did it arouse my astonishment. That is all. Nevertheless, each time I entered it, I never failed to be reminded of the absence of Buddha.

The SMR's remarkable achievement, like their central offices, was in realizing a grand ambition, based on a strong blending of all that was perceived as desirable from Japan and the West. But perhaps through the drive to become a central power, to become like a European nation, Meiji Japan was losing sight of its own character. Perhaps the marked absence of Buddha in the Great Hall – the absence that so forcibly strikes Sōseki – represents this missing conscience, or misplaced identity of Meiji Japan as it related to Manchuria. In fact, a series of lectures that Sōseki gave only two years later, in 1911, dealt precisely with the moral dangers involved in an overly aggressive pursuit of Westernization.

□

The *Asahi* Newspaper and the Reception of *Travels*

For English-speaking readers, it seems strange at first that Japan's foremost modern novelist published most of his writings in the *Asahi* newspaper – it seems odd especially for such an intellectual writer as Sōseki.[14] However, newspapers in Meiji Japan were quite different, both in audience and content, from the newspapers of today, including the *Asahi*. The *Asahi*, particularly its Tokyo branch, was an important vehicle for prose writers during the Meiji period (Fowler, 134), and it published all of Sōseki's fiction, including *Travels*, from mid-1907 until his death in 1916. According to Edward Fowler, who studied the newspaper as literary vehicle in Meiji Japan, the *Asahi* had a very small, élite circulation – about 100,000 in 1905, increasing to 110,000 in 1910, a year after *Travels* was printed, and then jumping to 420,000 by 1925. As numbers increased, the proportion of literary columns to news and editorial columns decreased. At the time when Sōseki was publishing in the *Asahi*, the front pages tended to be dominated by literature in serial form and some editorial essays. Political and international news was frequently found on the second or third page, and one often had to dig to page seven or so for local news. Travel essays, instalments of translated literature, long poems, and literary essays all tended to have higher billing than local news (Fowler, 135).

In the *Asahi*, Sōseki not only had his own daily column, where he serialized his fiction, but he also sponsored a second literary column, to which a range of talented authors contributed. Sōseki's contract with the *Asahi* is interesting in that he arranged for a kind of 'tenure', where the *Asahi* had no control over the content of his writings, as long as he promised to publish all his fiction with them, including at least one novel per year. *Travels* was published in 51 daily instalments starting only four days after Sōseki's return, and lasting until the end of December 1908. It seems odd in many ways that Sōseki chose to truncate his travelogue, despite the fact that he completely excluded the second country forming part of the title of his series: *Travels in Manchuria and Korea*. Judging by the notes he used to construct the travel narrative, he could have continued for at least 100 issues, rather than stopping at instalment number 51. Beongcheon Yu claims that it is unlikely that he stopped because the serial was unpopular, and that it just seemed 'unnatural' to continue past the end of the calendar year. However, Sōseki stopped just short of recounting his experiences of the coal mines and miners of Fushun. The visit must have been of great interest to him, given his novel *Kofu* (*The Miner*, 1908), in which he portrays the choice of a life as a miner as equivalent to suicide.

In the following sections, we will examine the two primary objections made to *Travels*: first, that Sōseki is shamefully blind to the politically charged scenes he is witnessing and second, that he is obsessed by himself, his school friends, and his nostalgic reminiscences as he travels through these exotic locales. In the process, we will also consider Sōseki's place in Meiji literature to help explain his unusual style of narration in *Travels*.

□

Political Controversy Over *Travels*

Many readers, Japanese as well as Western, have blamed Sōseki for his prejudicial attitude towards the Chinese in *Travels*. The most oft-cited instance of this is his use of the pejorative terms '*chan*' and '*rosuke*'. Readers may also be struck by the constant refrain regarding the poor hygiene of the Chinese and Manchurians he encounters. At times he seems to equate the Chinese with filth. For example, when he arrives in Dairen, the narrator says:

> On the pier, there were crowds of people; most of the people there, however, were Chinese coolies.[15] Looking at any one of them, I had the immediate impression of dirt. Any two gathered together were even a more unpleasant sight. That so many of them had gathered together struck me as most unwelcome indeed. Standing on the deck, I contemplated this mob from my distant observation point and thought to myself: 'Goodness! what a strange place I've gotten myself to!' (Chapter 4)

Passages such as these have led Joshua Fogel, for example, to remark that Sōseki was 'unable to transcend the prejudices of his time' (Fogel, 582). It has also led other critics to try to assess the nature of Sōseki's sarcasm, the relationship between the historical Sōseki and the narrator of *Travels*. To what extent are we supposed to consider the travelling narrator's opinions to be Sōseki's, or to what extent is he, as Ara Masato argues, building a flawed protagonist, just as he does in his novels *I am a Cat* and *Botchan*? It is difficult to arrive at any concrete conclusions to these questions;

however, it does seem clear that Sōseki directs sarcasm at his protagonist (or himself) as well as at the Chinese, as Fowler points out. It is also clear that there are strong fictional elements of *Travels*, and that the narrator is by no means identical to the historical Sōseki.

It is also not clear that Sōseki portrays any consistent opinion regarding the Chinese – instead, the narrator's opinion is marked by its ambivalence. For every negative remark regarding the Chinese, there is another scene that tends to balance the impression.[16] Beongcheon Yu notes Sōseki's portrayal in *Travels* of:

> ... the peacefulness of natives carrying bird cages, forgetful of their own hunger; the patience and energy of native coolies labouring in sweat; the haunting beauty of native girls of pleasure; and moving silhouettes of a blind musician and a little dancer, gentle outlines of the earth singularly reminiscent of Sung landscape paintings. (Yu, 90).

And while all these scenes do occur, Yu perhaps exaggerates the overall tone, for the scene with the dancer and musician, for example, does indeed 'move' the narrator, but it moves him to extreme physical disgust. Scenes of disgust are interspersed throughout the travelogue, but so are scenes of admiration and sympathy for the plight of the workers. The most striking example of sympathy is exhibited when Sōseki (narrator and protagonist) sees an old man who has had his leg torn open by a passing vehicle. When he sees the man sitting motionless on the street surrounded by a crowd of people, Sōseki suddenly is shaken from his detached stance of observer and has a desperate urge to intervene in the scene, to get help for the man. Ultimately, however, it is probably futile to try to tally the pro-Chinese passages against the anti-Chinese passages in *Travels*, for that is to reduce Sōseki's artistry to tabulation.

Rather than Sōseki's condescending remarks about the Chinese and Manchurians, it is actually his *omissions* that have engendered greater resentment in the West. James Fujii, for example, discusses Sōseki's 'lapses in critical perspective on Japan's presence in continental Asia' and criticizes him for his lack of 'sensitivity to conditions in which one nation is occupying another'. Fujii seems particularly to object to what Sōseki tends to omit, to forget, or not to notice in the first place. He claims it is 'not simply a matter of resurrecting Sōseki's embarrassing lapses or of how difficult it is to step outside of an imperialist ethos that formed quickly in post-Restoration Japan'; the issue is rather 'the collective memory loss in cultural production' (Fujii, 226). Beóngcheon Yu, although not drawing the same political conclusions, also speculates as to whether Sōseki's omissions are due to the 'unconscious elimination of unpleasantness', but finds her resolution in the fact that if Sōseki does not condemn, then he also does not eulogize (Yu, 89–90).[17]

Miyoshi Yukio has suggested yet another possible reason, both for the sudden halting of the serial, but also, by implication, for the political content of Sōseki's piece, given its audience and the historical moment. Miyoshi speculates that political events 'may well have confused Sōseki's feelings towards his subject and have intervened in his ability to continue his story'. During the time that Sōseki's serial was being published, widespread political outrage followed the assassination of Itō Hirobumi by a Korean secessionist. The *Asahi* newspaper article announcing the event was headlined 'Prince Itō was killed by a Korean!'. Miyoshi argues that, as a result, *Travels* changed suddenly 'from a comfortable travel journal to that of a highly charged political battleground':

> Ten days after the assassination, a vitriolic series appeared entitled 'Dreadful Korea'. For about one month, these series appeared side by side with *Travels*, and must have made Sōseki very uneasy. It may be that Sōseki took the excuse of the start of a new year to cease writing on this uncomfortably political subject, and decided to end his account before his arrival in Korea.[18]

Miyoshi's theory is supported by the fact that as soon as the series 'Dreadful Korea' began appearing, *Travels* was moved to a less prominent page. Although Miyoshi does not argue the point, it could be that Sōseki felt the need to appeal to his audiences even while he was writing the 'comfortable' travelogue. It is hard to imagine that the topic of Manchuria and the SMR could have been a 'comfortable' or neutral subject a mere three years after the settlement of the Russo-Japanese War, one year after the founding of the SMR, and one year before the official annexation of Korea. It is equally difficult to imagine that, given the daily appearance of this serial, that Sōseki would not have felt somewhat pressured to appeal to popular stereotypes of the Chinese and the Koreans.

What is particularly odd, though, about Sōseki's remarks in *Travels*, even when one takes the politically charged circumstances into account, is that he was generally known for his independence of mind, and even for his strong stance against the rampant nationalism around him. He often lectured on such topics in the years following the publication of *Travels,* defying the excesses of nationalism by ridiculing its extremes: 'Do we go to the toilet or wash our faces for our country?' (*Zenshu*, 14:379; McClellan,6), he asked. His 'tenure' at the *Asahi* also protected him from excessive pressure to succumb to public opinion; and he was known for his strong stances on the author's separation from public opinion. When he was voted the most popular author in Japan in the *Taiyō* Popularity Poll, for example, he refused the gold cup they offered him, again insisting on the separation between art and public opinion.

□

Sōseki's Non-Political Narrator

It is interesting to note that *Travels* opens with a criticism that could almost have come from contemporary readers, appalled by Sōseki's bland acceptance of the political situation in Manchuria:

> You know, it is interesting to go and have a look at what the Japanese are doing abroad. Guys like you who know nothing at all [i.e. authors] take a patronizing attitude and create misunderstandings. A tour will be just what you need (Chapter 1).

The irony here, from a modern perspective, is that the words are spoken by the chief officer of the infamous SMR – it is Zekō's criticism of the Sōseki-narrator. Zekō, too, is trying to rouse Sōseki to become more politically informed, to travel, observe, and take a political stance, although presumably not the one most readers would recommend today.

Such conscious manipulation of the narrator's image again suggests a literary dimension to *Travels* that has never been adequately accepted. Why is it that Sōseki would use this medium to create a fictional narrator-author who is markedly ignorant and detached from worldly concerns, who is dangerously non-political in highly political times? The very first words we hear from the narrator of *Travels* are: 'What exactly *is* the South Manchurian Railway Company anyway?' This could hardly have been a socially acceptable degree of ignorance of Japan's primary foreign investment, and was a particularly daring question to address to the President of the SMR. And of course, since Sōseki created this travel narrative based on notes of his trip, weeks after the events had occurred, he was consciously selecting what to include, what to emphasize. *Travels* is, in short, a travelogue or a travel narrative, rather than a travel diary.

In the course of the narrative, the Sōseki character frequently claims ignorance, forgets facts, names, words, and historical dates, all the while calling attention to his forgetfulness (e.g. 'Lieutenant So-and-So'). He also stresses his ignorance of and distance from worldly matters such as trains, dates, and schedules (Chapter 31). And he shows reluctance to go to any of the usual tourist destinations, such as the Bay at Port Arthur, scene of the first battle of the Russo-Japanese War. Most striking, perhaps, is the conversation that the Sōseki character has with Mr Kawamura, head of the Enquiry department at the SMR headquarters in Dairen. This visit, initiated by Zekō rather than Sōseki, could easily have taken place in one of Sōseki's novels with a socially awkward, adolescent hero, stumbling to say the right thing in an uncomfortable situation. He has no interest in inquiring into the workings of the SMR, and thinks only about the humorous embarrassment of the situation:

> Now that I, a highly learned and experienced man, had ended up in the Enquiry department, I felt highly embarrassed when he asked me in a grave tone to elaborate the direction of my inquiries. 'Er, well ...,' I began. ...

Sōseki then launches into excruciating explanations of his stomach discomfort and his efforts to disguise them. It almost seems that he uses stomach pains as an excuse for not learning or conveying more facts about the SMR. When Kawamura produces a large stack of volumes, Sōseki refuses to look through them, hitting upon the ingenious solution of asking for a broad sketch of the SMR's activities. The reader does not even receive this sketch, however, because an old school friend enters the room, and Sōseki's mind wanders to old reminiscences.

In scenes such as this, one cannot help but think that the absence of information about the SMR would have irritated Japanese audiences, curious about the events in Manchuria. It would seem, therefore, that the forgetfulness, absent-mindedness, and perplexing passivity of Sōseki's narrator in such scenes actually function as protection for Sōseki the author against the political pressures facing him, both from his audience, and from Zekō and the SMR. One could argue that, in this way, he actually takes something of a political stance against nationalist pressures to engage political issues.

☐

Meiji Literary Debates

In order to understand the relation of Sōseki's narrative techniques to Meiji literary culture, it will be helpful to take a look at some contemporary debates about the shape of the novel. As mentioned above, the Meiji Period was characterized by an almost ravenous appetite for things Western, manifested partly in the energetic cultural movement called *Bummeikaika* (or 'civilization and enlightenment'). After almost two centuries of closed borders and minimal contact with other cultures, as well as growing civil dissatisfaction (as George M. Wilson convincingly argues), many Japanese eagerly sought new patterns and ideals by imitating material features of the Western world. The resulting complex blend of xenophilia and xenophobia became one of the defining characteristics of the literary debates in this period, along with many other aspects of culture. In the dichotomous popular view, the West tended to represent things modern, especially individualism and advances in technology and science, while Japan stood for ancient tradition, stable community structure, and understanding of things spiritual or poetic. This dichotomy was reflected in the popular Meiji saying: '*Tōyō no dōtoku, Seiyō no geijitsu*' – Eastern soul, Western technology.

Meiji leaders debated whether it was possible to overcome this dichotomy through education – that is, to learn from the rational, scientific West without sacrificing the soulful, spiritual East. Even leaders who thought a synthesis of 'Eastern ethics and Western science' feasible, including Sakuma Shōzan, perpetuated these dichotomies through their characterizations of the divergent cultural strengths. Debates over the shape of the novel in this same Meiji culture were therefore also thinly veiled political debates over national identity as well as over Japan's place in relation to its expanding world, particularly *vis-à-vis* the 'West.' As Etō Jun writes:

> No matter how radically they differed from one another in their literary or political opinions, Meiji writers shared in the dominant national mission of their time: the creation of a new civilization that would bring together the best features of East and West, while remaining Japanese at its core (Etō, 603).

However, concern over the state and adequacy of the Japanese language extended far beyond literary critics. The debates that raged over the language of the novel figure within a larger debate over the relationship between language and civilization (modernization) and again suggest a crisis regarding national identity. In order to understand the degree of national self-questioning, one has to recognize that figures as prominent as the Minister of Education and the Japanese chargé d'affaires in Washington both seriously proposed the abolition of the Japanese language in favour of English (see Miyoshi, 5; Ryan, 64–66).

The writings of one of the most influential revolutionary Meiji literary critics, Tsuboichi Shōyō (1859–1935), forcefully promoted the 'Westernization' of Japanese literature by encouraging a shift towards 'tightly constructed plots with logical development'.[19] Futabatei Shimei's *Ukigumo* (*Floating Cloud,* 1889) is generally considered to be the first modern novel in Japan because (directly in response to Tsuboichi's teaching) it successfully blends the two aesthetics: it combines Western linearity with Japanese sequentiality, by creating one central unifying voice, whose authority is veiled by the fact that he ruminates and associates from scene to scene. In this way, this prominent Meiji author represents the self-conscious formation of narrative strategies and the mingling of two contrasting aesthetic systems to accord with a changing national identity.

Natsume Sōseki grew up surrounded by these cultural and aesthetic clashes between East and West. It was one year after the influential publication of *Ukigumo,* Japan's first 'Western' novel, that Sōseki became the first official student sponsored by the Japanese emperor Meiji to study English literature abroad. As we saw above, Sōseki felt deeply that he was representing his country abroad, for better or worse. He felt that his studies were a government mission, and knew that part of the purpose of the mission was to be able afterwards to replace the foreigners teaching English literature in Japan.[20] His sojourn in England clearly influenced Sōseki as a writer, for his writings after this period are packed with erudite allusions to many European authors, and even the form of his novels suggests the influence of his studies upon his own art. After his return, when Sōseki received his university position and became a pre-eminent literary figure of the Meiji period, he too, like his predecessors Tsuboichi and Futabatei, helped define the new direction and 'Westernization' of the Japanese novel and his own response to 'Western linearity'.[21]

Sōseki balances his knowledge of the Western novel and its narrative techniques against the 'sequentiality' of the traditional Japanese literary diary, which, according to Maria Flutsch, 'celebrated personal experience and valued the intensity of subjective reaction to events in life.' These diaries were based on an understanding of experience that emphasized its ephemerality:

'Since all existence is transient and time flows away like a river, life and experience flow with it like the bubbles on the surface. The greater the awareness of ephemerality of an experience, the deeper that intensity of feeling it aroused.' (Flutsch, 13). He was also influenced by the *shaseibun* tradition, championed by his poet-mentor Masaoka Shiki (1867–1902). *Shaseibun* showed a similar distrust of consciousness, rational control, and closure, and emphasized the idea of sketching verbal pictures from life, as in *haiku*. In *Travels*, we see elements of these influences. They stand in interesting tension with the linearity of the SMR train itself: perhaps the modern predicament is expressed by the difficulty one encounters trying to be a poet-wanderer while also keeping an eye on the train schedule.

□

Pain, Passivity and the Colour of Manchuria

As regards Sōseki's non-political narrator, it is helpful to consider Sōseki's own perceptions of the nature of literature, as he describes it in another seldom read work, his *Theory of Literature* (*Bungaku hyōron*, 1909). In this work, published in the same year as *Travels*, Sōseki defines literature as non-political and non-ethical. He says that human beings have three main faculties – intellect, emotion and will – and that the artist's domain is the second alone:

> [T]hose who apply intellect ... are people who elucidate the interrelationships of things; they are labelled philosophers and scientists. Those who apply emotion are people who taste the interrelationships of things; they are known as artists and men of letters. Those who apply will are people who improve the interrelationships of things; they are called warriors, statesmen, beancake makers, carpenters, and so forth (Ueda, 6).

Thus, an artist must by definition separate himself from the rational and the utilitarian. He also criticizes Jonathan Swift for being too political and not adequately poetic in *Gulliver's Travels*: 'a world traveller like Gulliver should have enjoyed the colours of the ocean, the sound of the waves, the sight of flying birds, etc'.[22] Sōseki's own travelogues, whether of travel in Asia or London, did avoid political relevance, and therefore, by his own definition, achieve a more literary character. Sōseki's travelogues from his time in England, such as *The Tower of London*, are similarly detached from the present, from politics, and from the living people around him. There, too, he dwells on his own feelings and on the past (albeit England's past, rather than his schooldays). It may be,

28

therefore, that the politically charged context of *Travels* intensified his pre-existing sense of the importance of the separation of politics and art.

These arguments also help explain the obsessive interest Sōseki displays, in *Travels*, in his own emotions, and particularly in his stomach discomforts. In retrospect, the trip to Manchuria was actually the first of many bouts Sōseki would have with stomach ulcers; it was his first experience of the illness that gradually worsened until it caused his death seven years later. Dissatisfied readers, even among Sōseki's contemporaries, have given *Travels* the nickname *Sōseki tokoro dokoro* (literally 'Sōseki Here and There' instead of 'Here and There in Manchuria and Korea'). The substitution of Sōseki's name for the destinations suggests that Sōseki could have been anywhere, since he pays no attention to his surroundings. Yet, Sōseki said: 'My method is always to analyse my own psychological phenomena. For me that explains things most satisfactorily . . .' (*Zenshu* 31:7–8).

In light of this emphasis on passivity and emotion, it is worth revisiting the title of the piece translated here. Its Japanese name, *Mankan tokoro dokoro*, literally means 'here and there in Manchuria and Korea', and has a careless, carefree tone that suggests wandering rather than travelling. It suggests the lack of an itinerary, the lack of wilful control, or rational planning. Similarly, Sōseki's *Omoidasu kotonado* (generally translated as *Recollections*) literally means 'remembering and so forth', also de-emphasizing the active role that 'recollecting' suggests. In other words, here as in other of his works, Sōseki is eager to de-emphasize the role of the will in his artistry. This may be another way of explaining his constant refrains about his passivity, his laziness, and his illness in *Travels*. In fact, the people in *Travels* who reveal zest, energy, or curiosity are usually portrayed as foolish or rustic, such as Zekō with his zest for outings to Western-style events, Shirani with his healthy appetite for food, and Hashimoto with his eagerness to make plans and see sights. It is in the suspension of the will and in absorption with emotions that Sōseki seems to find the opportunity to let images succeed one another, invoking a series of emotions in the reader as well. Perhaps the most interesting example of this occurs in Chapter 38, where he watches the Manchurian horizon darken and images float by the train window, until the shapes begin to take on a life of their own in his imagination, beyond his power to control them. The clouds transform themselves into a great wall, and telephone poles become people moving busily along the top of the wall until he awakens from his dreamlike state.

Sōseki seems to have taken a lesson from his reading of *Gulliver's Travels*, and pays a great deal of attention to the colour of the sky in the course of *Travels*. In fact, as the narrative progresses, he tends to end more and more chapters with ruminations on the majesty of the landscape before him. Chapters 25, 32, 33, 36, and 49 all end with expansive vistas, some with comparisons to Chinese paintings. As in his novels, Sōseki tends to use colours to paint emotions, and in Manchuria he frequently returns to the brilliant reds and sorghum yellows of the landscape. It is interesting that it is really only in such vistas that Sōseki seems to find tranquillity, and also the ability to admire Manchuria. He admires its vast expanses, its occasional fertility, and finds in these moments his only occasions for positive comparisons with Japan: the sun is brighter in Manchuria than in Japan, he exclaims, and the air is clearer as well. Perhaps it is only when viewing these vistas that Sōseki can forget the tension between Western technology and Japanese souls long enough to appreciate an Asian neighbour who does not so neatly fit into the dichotomous thinking that was so widespread during the Meiji Era.[23]

NOTES

1 I will follow the tradition of referring to Natsume Sōseki by his pen name. In the case of Sōseki, Natsume is actually his family name and Kinnosuke his given name. All other Japanese names will be given in the traditional order of family name first, and I will refer to these authors and political figures in shorthand by their family names. Contemporary American critics with Japanese names will be referred to with the surname last.

2 A lightweight summer kimono, worn by both sexes. It is usually made of cotton.

3 While Sōseki is the only Japanese author to have a museum dedicated to his works located outside Japan (Sōseki Museum, London, founded by Sammy Tsunematsu), this museum is visited primarily by Sōseki scholars and by Japanese tourists.

4 There are many interesting parallels between Sterne and Sōseki. Not only was Sōseki the first to translate and write about Sterne in Japan ('On Tristram Shandy', 1897), but Sterne also appears in *Three-Cornered World*. Also, Sōseki might have found it humorous that, just as Sterne composed a work entitled *A Sentimental Journey through France and Italy*, in which the narrator-protagonist never reaches Italy, Sōseki's narrator-protagonist also never reaches Korea in *Travels in Manchuria and Korea*.

5 Sōseki distinguished himself early on in his studies and excelled in his studies of classical Chinese, and particularly his ability at *kanshi*, poems in the classical Chinese format. In fact, he is still considered by many to be the best Japanese author of *kanshi* of the past several centuries.

6 For an excellent selection of such prints, see Meech-Pekarik.

7 Quoted in Field, 265.

8 Most critics and general readers are acquainted with his trip to London and ignore his travels within Asia. James Fujii claims that this is a sign of collective ignoring or forgetting of Japanese colonial aggressions: 'the collective memory loss in cultural production' (Fujii, 226).

9 It is debatable how industrialized Russia was at this point, but, from a Meiji perspective, it was Western and therefore by definition industrialized.

10 This context of complex Asian relations must be remembered when Sōseki's narrator reacts with such discomfort and anxiety to a Westerner asking him his nationality wondering: 'what other nationalities he had considered for me' (Chapter 6).

11 SMR propaganda books, such as *Modern Manchuria*, put it this way: 'Most of these hotels are operated entirely as a facility to travellers, as they are conducted at a heavy loss, the deficit for 1927 being thus ¥336,800' (Kinney, 40).

12 Duus uses the term 'informal empire' to contrast with Japan's 'formal empire': colonial possessions, such as Korea, won directly through territorial conquest.

13 The '*tatami*' is a padded straw mat measuring ca. 1.8 × 0.9 metres in area and half a centimetre in thickness, with a darker border along the two long sides. *Tatami* mats cover most rooms in the traditional Japanese house, particularly reception rooms and private rooms. Because of their standardized size, they provide even today a common way of calculating the area of the rooms in homes and apartments.

14 The most analogous situation in the West would be the nineteenth-century serial publishing of prose fiction, such as the novels of Charles Dickens.

15 The word Sōseki uses here is *rosuke*, which is itself an interesting word choice since its presumed derivation is from the word 'Russkii' – it originally seems to be a derogatory name for Russians rather than the Chinese (*Kōjien*).

16 Sōseki would probably regard such ambivalence or inconsistency as a sign of artistic success, judging by his remarks on the notion of the self in his writing on literary criticism:

> Novelists often talk proudly about 'describing a character like this' or 'creating a character like that.' . . . But they are only enjoying writing [. . .] lies. To speak the truth, there is nothing coherent that you could call a 'character'. Novelists can't write reality, and even if they could, it would not make a novel. Real people are strangely difficult to make 'coherent' (Sōseki, *Zenshu*, III:441).

Incoherence is a central feature of humanity for Sōseki. Contradictions in motivation, in action, and in speech are essential to his portrayals in *Kokoro* and, indeed, in most of his novels (Matsui, 52).

17 If Sōseki's letters are to be trusted, then it is interesting that he expresses so *little* admiration for the Japanese efforts in Manchuria within *Travels*. His letters express much greater admiration than does the narrator of *Travels*: 'As I travelled around Manchuria and Korea, I really felt as though the Japanese are indeed a trustworthy people'; 'Japanese are vigorously engaged in activities all over Manchuria, and these activities are just remarkable. I thought that the Japanese were really something' (Takeuchi 296–99).

18 Miyoshi Yukio, 245–46. Ironically, it was Itō's face that Sōseki replaced on the ¥1000 bill.

19 See Miner, *Genesis*, 349–350; Ryan, 38; and Brodey, 'Literary Linearity' for further discussion of these ideas.

20 After returning to Japan and receiving a position as Instructor at the Imperial University, Sōseki had the awkward task of replacing the very popular Lafcadio Hearn (the subject of another volume in the *Rediscovering* series). Interestingly, both Hearn and Sōseki had earlier taught at the same school on the island of Kyushu: Kumamoto Higher Middle School.

21 See Brodey, 'Literary Linearity' for more on Sōseki's response to these debates and his relation to the narrative style of Laurence Sterne, as well as a discussion of the issues involved with self-narration and self-representation.

22 Quoted in Ueda, 12.

23 I would like to acknowledge my gratitude for the generous collaboration of Sammy I. Tsunematsu and Hans Bjarne Thomsen, as well as the useful suggestions from Suzanne Barnett and Barak Kushner, and the encouragement of Bill Sibley and Norma Field, and the editorial assistance of Breanne Goss.

Travels in Manchuria and Korea

By Natsume Sōseki

Translated and Edited by
INGER SIGRUN BRODEY and SAMMY I. TSUNEMATSU

1

'What exactly is the South Manchurian Railway Company anyway?' In reply to my perfectly serious question, the President of the Railway Company[1] looked slightly disgusted and replied: 'Old boy, you really are a fool!'

Being called an idiot by Zekō [see Plate 1] didn't particularly bother me, so I felt no need to reply. Rather dreamily, he then suggested: 'What do you say to our taking a tour together?'

It had been many years since Zekō had suggested taking me anywhere. When he was twenty-five, he had taken me to a cheap cafeteria in Kanda,[2] just opposite the Ogawa Restaurant where one could get a variety of fried dishes[3] and, ever since then, he had from time to time taken it into his head to suggest going places. But never before had he suggested taking me to such a startling place as this. 'His offer to go somewhere with me will be just like every other time', I said to myself, replying with only an indistinct grunt.

On hearing such a vague reply, the President continued: 'You know, it is interesting to go and have a look at what the Japanese are doing abroad. Guys like you who know nothing at all take patronizing attitudes and create misunderstandings. A tour will be just what you need.'

Asking Zekō about various matters, I learned, among other things, that he had left a generous tip at the hotel in Shimonoseki.[4] Most of us generally consider such a gesture pointless. Accompanying Zekō would give me an opportunity to observe the impact of enormous tips on hotel owners, servants and grooms. So I made the following proposal: 'While travelling with you, I would want to see a number of different places, and would be interested in seeing anything you wish to show me.'

He said that that was not a problem and saw no reason why we should not travel separately if I had any objection to our travelling together.

I then wondered when it would be possible for him to accompany me. I was waiting, never actually believing such a trip would materialize, when, in mid-August, a member of his staff came to Tokyo and asked me whether I could be ready to depart at a moment's notice. I replied that my profession left me free to depart as soon as he gave me the word. About ten days later, I received a letter from him announcing the sailing date of a ship leaving Shimonoseki and asking me whether that was convenient. I told him it was perfectly fine; however, shortly afterwards, I received another letter from him, this time asking me whether I was willing to put it off until the following sailing, because of a last-minute business transaction. I had no trouble in agreeing to the delay.

Just at that time, however, I suffered an attack of acute gastritis. As a result, I – who have always taken great pride in keeping my word – found it very difficult to say for certain whether or not I would be well enough to travel by the proposed departure date. When a spasm came on, promises no longer counted. Shimonoseki, gratuities, Zekō, Dairen[5] – all these prospects disappeared into thin air. The entire universe seemed like one jet-black mass. Somewhat concealed beneath the surface, however, my interest in this journey of ours persisted. There was certainly no question of suggesting to Zekō that he leave me behind.

My stomach was filled with a sort of gas. The tinkling of a mug of tea filled me with fury. Why do people eat? They are animals who act contrary to reason. There is nothing wrong with just sucking ice cubes. Ice is innocence itself – and more than sufficient. Such, at least, was my impression at that moment. If someone at my bedside spoke to me, I felt he was a despicable and vulgar creature who obviously could not live without chattering. On opening my eyes, I glanced at the shelves and saw they were stacked full of books. Every volume had its own colour, and they all had different titles. There were so many of them that it left me quite bewildered. Had someone in a moment of madness made them all so different? How had Fate succeeded in juxtaposing all those titles, making them look so important? I was sunk in an unimaginably suffocating atmosphere. I wished I would die.

Teiji[6] approached my bed and asked how I was. I did not know what answer to give him because it seemed idiotic to reply at all.

The assistant doctor, stepping in for my regular practitioner, came over to examine me and said there could be no thought of my undertaking any journey in such a condition.

'As a doctor, I forbid you to go,' he admonished me.

Agreeing with him and contradicting him would have been equally repugnant to me.

During this period, the days passed inexorably by. The illness continued to plague me in the same places. At last, the eve of our proposed departure arrived and I telephoned Nakamura to cancel my part in it. He wished me a speedy recovery and embarked alone.

2

As I was leaving the steamship company and boarding the *Tetsureimaru*,[7] Mr Okohira of the steamship company said to me: 'I was told you were travelling with the President.'

After the vessel had started on its voyage, the purser remarked to me: 'I had understood you would be on board the same ship as the President.'

When I met the captain at the entrance to the saloon, he said: 'Somebody told me you would be making the crossing in the company of the President. Is that true?'

With everyone it was 'President this' and 'President that'. All of a sudden I felt afraid to call him 'Zekō'. I had to reply:

'Yes, yes! I had planned to travel in the company of the President. Yes, I had an appointment with the President, to go on the same boat.'

I suddenly became very sparing in the use of the name Zekō, which I had been using for the past five years. This self-censorship started aboard the *Tetsureimaru* and continued, from Dairen onwards, throughout the whole of Manchuria, as I crossed the province of Andong[8] and finally reached Korea. But neither did I know how to use the word 'President' in the presence of the others. This title that now belonged to my old friend Zekō Nakamura, was too distinguished, too conspicuous, and insufficiently intimate: it was totally devoid of charm. Despite my wish to stop calling him Zekō, the name that I had used for so long and to which I wanted sole access, I found it most regrettable that fear of others' opinions was causing me to treat an intimate friend like a stranger for fifty days.

Life on the ship was fairly pleasant. Having set sail from Kobe on the day after the two-hundred-and-tenth day of spring (according to the lunar calendar),[9] I naturally feared a high wind and a stormy crossing. Contrary to my expectations, however, the weather was good. From Kobe to Dairen, the sea resembled a vast expanse of smooth oil. When I tell you that a young Englishman was able to sleep peacefully on the top deck holding a dog in his arms, you will easily be able to picture the calm state of the sea.

I asked the purser, Mr Saji: 'Who is that over there?'

'I've heard he's the British Vice Consul,' he replied.

Vice Consul or not, to me he was just a nice-looking young man of twenty-one or twenty-two. On the other hand, his dog's countenance was as strange as could be. As a bulldog, it already had an unusual face by virtue of its breed. It may be cruel to persecute a dog with insults, but there was no getting round the fact that its head was indeed bizarrely shaped. Later, after we had put in at Dairen, the same young man entered the Hotel Yamato.[10] In the course of the meal in the elegant dining-room, my gaze inadvertently met the dog's and I started in surprise.

It was certainly not a dining-room where dogs should have been welcome. I had the impression that the dog had entered it by mistake. It was, however, accompanied by its master. The latter, apparently feeling that talking aloud to his bulldog in a crowded place would show a lack of good breeding, suddenly seized it round its middle and, carrying it pressed tightly against him, beat a highly elegant retreat. He reached the door with exemplary strides, passing silently between the tables at which large numbers of guests were seated. Carrying his dog, he held the awkward and heavy load with as much ease as if he had been carrying a *furoshiki*,[11] and disappeared. The bulldog emitted neither a single yelp nor any other sound. Like some limp, elastic apparatus, it meekly allowed itself be carried away. One would have thought it had been moved by natural forces. As I have already mentioned several times, this dog had an extraordinary face; there was nonetheless a kind of majesty in its demeanour at this moment. I never had the chance to see that face again.

3

Feeling bored, I went out on to the deck and looked into the distance.

The weather was changeable – now overcast, now clear – and the black silhouettes of smoke drifted upwards, seemingly to soil the peaceful sky. I spent a few moments watching the traces of smoke on the horizon and then sat down in a cane chair. On this particular day, the young Englishman had tethered his dog to the foot of his chair and was reading a book. He had stretched out his legs above his dog. In the lounge, another foreign passenger was busily drafting a letter. His wife was absent – perhaps gone to another part of the boat. The American missionary couple had moved to quarters near the captain's cabin. On the deck, the customary tranquillity prevailed. Only the ship's engines vibrated noisily beneath us, lulling me into a doze.

After waking up, I entered the lounge and chose an American magazine from a pile of periodicals; next to them there were also five or six Japanese magazines. Every periodical bore the seal 'Saji Library'. Mr Saji, the purser, explained to me that he bought magazines to read whenever the vessel put in at a port and that after he had read them, he presented them to the *Tetsureimaru*'s library. He apparently took great interest in literature. Among other things, he had read what I had written myself.[12] He told me that he came from the same place as one of my friends, Kuroyanagi Kaishu,[13] and we talked a little about what people said of him.

Once again, I left the lounge and looked out at the sea. I immediately noticed that a vessel that I had seen moving at a distance had come much closer, continuing to throw its black shadow on the waves. Its size, it seemed to me, was comparable to that of the *Tetsureimaru*. The ship was moving so slowly that before long we would, no doubt, overtake it. With my elbow resting on the handrail and my chin on my hand, I watched as the *Tetsureimaru* rapidly gained on the other ship. Finally, I was able to make out three yellow characters quite clearly: '*Eikomaru*'. Very soon, the bow of our boat passed the stern of the other ship. We gradually moved forwards until we were even with its middle. The two vessels, about a hundred metres apart, then proceeded almost parallel to each other.

Seven or eight minutes later, it seemed that the *Tetsureimaru* would have overtaken the *Eikomaru;* however, the distance between us, which I had estimated at about a hundred metres, had noticeably decreased. It was now possible to count the exact number of figures standing on the other vessel's deck. A careful look told me that they were all Westerners. Some of them raised their binoculars in order to take a look at us. But soon there was no longer any point in using them. The vessels came so close to each other that the people on the decks could see one another quite clearly, even to the point of distinguishing hair colour and facial features. When the black hull of the *Eikomaru* loomed up less than two metres from my eyes, I said to myself: 'Oh, Heavens! We're going to ram it!' I caught sight of the other vessel's bow, and it seemed almost to touch my eyes. Yet we moved closer still. Finally, we struck it violently on the slant, on a level with the second-class deck. At the same moment, two lifeboats suspended on the deck overturned, and the metal bars securing them were twisted out of shape. The crew of the *Eikomaru* applauded and shouted. A foreigner standing near me uttered a few words in a strange voice, among which I recognized the word 'Damn!'

An hour later Mr Saji sought me out:

'Mr Natsume,' he said, 'In this expression "skilfully avoid", what is the best way of writing the character "avoid"'?[14]

'Er, well . . .', I began.

The fact is, I must confess that I did not know myself. Struggling for an answer, I told him that the character 'change', found in the expression 'change currency' might be suitable. However, because I had not given a reply quite worthy of a man of letters, my interlocutor looked perplexed – dubious, in fact.

'But that character,' he said, 'is used when it's a question of exchanging objects, isn't it?'

For want of a better solution, I advised him to transcribe this character into the phonetic syllabary.[15] Mr Saji, overcome with astonishment, took his leave. On asking him about it a little while later, I learned that he had intended to use the phrase in his official report: 'Our vessel skilfully avoided the danger.'

4

The steamer came alongside a stone wharf that reminded me of the one at Iida [see Plate 19].[16] It did so with such precision that I should never have believed I was at sea. On the pier, there were crowds of people; most of the people there, however, were Chinese coolies.[17] Looking at any one of them, I had the immediate impression of dirt. Any two together were an even more unpleasant sight. That so many of them had gathered together struck me as most unwelcome indeed. Standing on the deck, I contemplated this mob from my distant observation point and thought to myself: 'Goodness! What a strange place I've come to!'

As the boat approached the landing stage, people began to greet their acquaintances by waving their hats in the direction of the shore. The wife of the missionary, whose name was Wing, laughingly asked me, in a tone tinged with flattery:

'Perhaps Mr Nakamura has come to welcome you?'

But since I had sent no communication in advance, it would have been absurd to imagine that even the President, despite the privileges of his status, could have known of my impending arrival when I had not given him the date. I returned to my perch, again supporting myself by my elbows on the railing and resting my chin on my hand. 'And now, what on earth am I to do?' I asked myself. 'For now, I'll find Zekō and ask him for the name of a hotel. And then I'll book myself in there.'

While these thoughts were going through my head, the steamer passed alongside the shore in a calm and dignified manner, skimming close by that curious throng of coolies, and finally coming to a halt. As soon as we had docked, the crowd of coolies started buzzing and swarming like angry wasps. Their completely unexpected clamour partially deprived me of courage. 'But after all, I am fated to step on shore sooner or later and in the end somebody will certainly attend to me!' I told myself. I continued looking at the surging multitude, resting my elbow on the railing and my head in my hand. Then Mr Saji came up to me and enquired: 'Mr Natsume, where will you go now?'

I replied that, for starters, I was thinking of going to see the President. At that moment, an elegant gentleman in a dark blue summer suit approached me. He took a visiting card out of his pocket and greeted me politely. It was Mr Numata, a professional secretary. This was a great piece of luck for me. Still gazing at the noisy crowd, my elbows on the railing, my hand supporting my chin, I learned that Mr Numata had come on board to meet and take home an elderly person from our native country. Having been given to understand that I was also on board the *Tetsureimaru*, he pointedly handed me his visiting card.

'Well, is the gentleman going to take the hotel's horse carriage?' he enquired, addressing Saji.

I looked along the pier and noticed the horse carriages drawn up on the landing place. There were also a large number of rickshaws. However, they were pulled by the same crowd of bellowing men, so business did not appear, compared with Japan at least, to be particularly good; most of the horse carriages also seemed to be operated by the same people. Consequently, all that was there was a load of dirty vehicles clanking away. Of the horse carriages in particular it had been rumoured, at the time when the Russkis[18] had evacuated Dairen during the Russo-Japanese War, that the Chinese had very carefully dug holes and buried the vehicles in order to prevent their falling into Japanese hands. Afterwards, the Chinks[19] walked about everywhere sniffing the ground; when they found the right smell, they noisily disinterred one carriage, then another, in the same manner. Very soon, Dairen was teeming with growling, muttering diggers of holes. These, of course, were just rumours, and I do not know what really happened. In any event, of all the rumours circulating from that time, this seems one of the cleverest, and anybody could see with his own eyes that these carriages were indeed covered in mud.

Among them there were two that stood out as conspicuously new and elegant. Even in the very heart of Tokyo, one could not easily have found their like. The coachmen, clad in elegant liveries and wearing shiny boots, held the reins of big plump Harbin[20] horses and waited in readiness to start on their journey. Saji left the vessel, going down the gangway to the wharf. He elbowed his way through the vociferous crowd and accompanied me personally to one of the elegant carriages. He invited me to get in, then turned to the coachman and gave him the President's address. The coachman immediately clutched his whip and the carriage set off in the midst of all the hullabaloo.

5

After passing through a gateway, the carriage drove over a gravel path for five or six metres and came to a gentle stop in front of a large porch. I mounted a flight of stone steps, and when I reached the entrance a servant girl of some fourteen or fifteen years of age, dressed in white, looked at me through the opening in the sturdy oak door, and saluted. I asked her whether the President had returned.

'No, the master is not here yet,' she replied.

So he was absent. 'A pity!' I wondered what I was now going to do. Standing on the steps, perplexed, I nodded my head. Then, thinking I heard footsteps behind me, I turned round and saw Mr

Numata, whom I had met just a few moments before, aboard the
Tetsureimaru.

'Well, please do come in!' he said.

I entered the house. Mr Numata preceded me and opened a
thick door at the end of the hallway. When I cast a glance through
the opening and surveyed the room beyond, I noticed that it was
astonishingly vast. Figures are not my forte, but even if I had
known the exact number of *tatami* mats it would have taken to fill
that room, it still would not have conveyed its majesty.[21] It made
me think of a sanctuary in a Buddhist temple, or of an entire
building constructed to a great length. In this great Japanese-style
drawing-room, one single carpet covered the *tatami* mats. Only the
four corners of the room contrasted with the carpet, which was
only a shade lighter in colour than the mats themselves and
emanated a faint glow. Chairs and tables for entertaining guests had
been placed on two different areas of this great carpet. The two
tables stood as far apart from each other as drawing-rooms would
have been in two adjacent houses. Numata guided me to a table
and showed me where to sit. Looking up, I saw that the ceiling was
extremely high. Considering the size of the room, this was in no
way surprising.

On entering the reception lounge, one found oneself on a level
with the first floor; from the balustrade one could survey the
ground floor. In other words, the ceiling above me was shared by
both the ground floor and the first floor. It was not until later on,
listening to the people's explanations, that I learned that this room,
which really was too vast for a reception lounge, actually served as
a dance hall. On such occasions, the ground floor, which was
visible below the balustrade, housed the orchestra.[22] Having said
this, however, I should have felt more at ease had I been informed
of this earlier: I would not have been so baffled at being suddenly
taken, without warning, into the sanctuary of a temple from which
Buddha was absent. During my stay in Dairen, I passed through
this hall several times in order to reach Zekō's office. Only once,
on the first visit, did it arouse my astonishment. That is all.
Nevertheless, each time I entered it, I never failed to be reminded
of the absence of Buddha.

On entering the room, one found windows on the right-hand
side, offering a view of life on the street. To the left, starting from
the middle of the hall, there hung a long curtain, serving to
partition off the adjacent room. Facing me, there were two potted
dwarf trees, or *bonsai*,[23] about a metre-and-a-half high. A pretty
ornament in the shape of an elephant the size of a piglet had been
placed by their side. I had seen exactly the same thing in the

lounge of the Railway Company's branch at Manihana, Tokyo.[24] They must have originally formed a pair, I thought to myself. A large panel of calligraphy had also been attached to the long curtain: 'Shimpei Gōtō,[25] President of the South Manchurian Railway Company' appeared in small characters on the left-hand edge. On examining the style of writing, I observed that the characters were painted with amazing evenness and were identical to those one could see on the shop signs in the Shanghai region. I admired the wonderful quality of Mr Gōtō's writing, perhaps acquired since arriving in Manchuria. In actual fact, however, the calligraphy I admired was not Mr Gōtō's, but the work of the Emperor of China.[26] I had not noticed the character for 'presented to' appearing just to the right of Gōtō's title. The characters of his name were really far too small. If Mr Gōtō actually had, through some extraordinary stroke of luck, met the Emperor of China in person, he must have found it difficult to tolerate having his name written in such small characters – and not even receiving any honorific title. It occurred to me that it might be preferable not to receive presents from such eminent personages.

Mr Numata called the servant and asked her to telephone everyone. Still, there was no trace of Zekō. A squadron of American naval men had dropped anchor in the port, and a baseball match was being organized in their honour. From the telephone conversation, it seemed that very probably Zekō must have attended this match.

In the end, darkness fell on the great hall.

'Well, suppose I look for a hotel?' I suggested. 'I will wait for him there.'

'As the Hotel Yamato is one of the Company's hotels, I think it would certainly be a very good choice,' replied Mr Numata, who very kindly escorted me there [see Plate 17].

6

A bath had been prepared for me. It was a long time since I had bathed in soft, fresh water, and I stretched out in it. In the midst of this repose, I heard a knock at the door. Since I had never before received a visit while bathing, I raised myself slightly, wondering what attitude to adopt. The person who had knocked was apparently intent on paying me this courtesy call, and once again I heard a persistent tapping at the door. It nevertheless seemed impossible to get right out of the bath stark naked.[27] But, as the knocking continued unabated, I decided to find out the reason for this visit before opening the door, so, sopping wet, I shouted:

'Hello! What is it?'

Then, on the other side of the frosted glass, someone said: 'Come on! Open the door for a second!'

I recognized the caller's voice and no longer saw any objection to opening the door. Stark naked and dripping with water, I turned the knob. As I had assumed, Zekō was standing in the threshold, walking stick in hand. 'Since you had decided to come, surely you could have sent me a wire, couldn't you?' he said.

'But what about you? Where did you go to?' I asked him.

'I went to a baseball match and then I had some business to attend to.'

Such were the salutations we exchanged.

'After you've dined, come to the house!' he said, offering to act as my guide.

'Agreed!' I replied, as I started to close the door again, adding: 'Tell me, the rules must be rather strict here. I'm probably not allowed to walk about in the hotel in a *yukata*, am I?'[28]

'You know, if it doesn't suit you here, you would do better to go to the Hotel Ryōto,'[29] he retorted, leaving me to return to his home.

At the agreed time, I went to the dining-room and had my meal at the table to which I was directed and in the company of a Westerner whom I did not know.

'Excuse me!' the man said, 'I fear I can't stop sneezing.'

He put a handkerchief to his nose. But I heard no sneeze.

'Go ahead! Go ahead!' I said, extending a half-spoken invitation to sneeze.

He told me he was English. Then he asked whether I had ever been to Port Arthur.[30]

'If you haven't, I'll explain everything to you: what train to take, what places to visit, and the best train for your return journey to Dairen.'

He recounted his own experience in detail. Listening to him, I punctuated his discourse with responses such as: 'Oh, really? Very interesting!' He then asked me whether I had ever been to Moji.[31]

'There's not much coal down there, is there?'

'That's true. There's hardly any,' I said.

In actual fact, I was completely ignorant as to whether that region was rich in coal or not.[32]

A few moments later, he put yet another question to me:

'Have you ever been to Port Arthur?' – the same question he had asked me just moments before.

His curious style of interrogation caused me some unease.

'No, no, not so far!' I answered, giving the same reply as before. He then explained all over again, in exactly the same manner as the first time, how best to manage the journey to Port Arthur:

'There are two trains one can take. One leaves at eight in the morning and the other at eleven.'

As before, I interjected 'Oh, really? Very interesting!' He ended by asking me, all of a sudden, whether I was Japanese.

'Yes,' I confirmed, quite openly, wondering with some anxiety what other nationality he had considered for me.[33]

As soon as I told him I was Japanese, the man said he had been to Yokohama forty years earlier.

'The Japanese are certainly polite, warm, and courteous. They're really a model nation!' he added, starting to overwhelm me with compliments. It seemed a pity to leave him at this juncture. But, since I had an appointment with Zekō, I brought the conversation with the old man to an end and took my leave.

As I emerged into the pleasant night air, the acacia leaves were motionless and silent; the foot-steps of passers-by could be heard along the distant pavement. A Westerner in a white suit, riding in a horse-drawn carriage, appeared out of the darkness. He was probably on his way back to the hotel. From the sound of the footsteps that followed, I guessed he had come to a stop in front of the porch. A high narrow tower rose from the centre of the roof of Zekō's villa, blackening part of the deep blue, almost violet, sky. In this early Dairen autumn, beyond the depths of the canopy overhead, the sky had taken on an intense colour nowhere to be found in Japan, and the stars were shining so brightly that one could have counted them one by one. . . .

7

A few days earlier, four warships belonging to the American Navy had arrived in the harbour. In the days that followed, a different event was organized daily, and entertainment was provided as well. The next evening a ball was scheduled, and Zekō suggested we should attend it.

'Go along to it, you say? But I haven't brought an evening suit with me. I couldn't possibly go!' I replied, rejecting his suggestion.

'You really are a spoilsport! One can't take you anywhere!' he retorted.

I remembered that when I was staying in London doing research, I had had the cheapest possible evening suit made for me at a shabby tailor's on Tottenham Court Road.[34] Since then it had always remained at the back of the wardrobe and even my closest friends did not know that I owned one. Even though Dairen might turn out to be a place where one dressed well, it had never occurred to me when I left Tokyo that this old evening suit might be useful in any way, and the back of the wardrobe was where it remained when I went abroad.

'Listen, I'll lend you a *hakama* and a *haori*[35] of my own and we will go in Japanese costume. It will be interesting to see what it's like!' said Zekō, who seemed to want to get me to that ball at all costs. I had not wanted to tell him that if it was a ball that we were going to, it would be silly not to dance and that if we wore Japanese clothes we would be unable to do so. But as Zekō was a very simple, uncomplicated man,[36] I was afraid to offend him by acquiescing to his suggestion in these terms, so instead I simply turned him down, saying that the *haori* and *hakama* were really not suitable. However, Zekō, apparently still very anxious to take me to this ball, buttonholed young Ueda on the first floor, towards the middle of the next day, saying: 'Tell me, would you care to lend this fellow your evening suit? It seems to me you're exactly the same size.'

Faced with such a sudden enquiry, Ueda might easily have appeared embarrassed. He laughingly put on a show of modesty: 'No, no! Nobody's my size!'

That was the end of our plan to go to the ball. A little while later, however, Zekō resumed his efforts: 'Suppose I take you to the Club?'[37]

Once again, he was offering to take me somewhere. I thought to myself that it was already quite late. But Kunizawa, who was there, said he, too, was prepared to go. We all three then went out into the cool evening, lit by electric street-lamps. After covering a hundred or two hundred metres, we came within sight of Nihonbashi Bridge. People called it the 'Japan Bridge'. It was such an elegant and robust structure that one could really have imagined oneself in the heart of Europe.[38] We entered a brick building just before reaching the bridge.

'Will there still be anyone there?' we wondered. We looked into the billiard room and found the lights on. But there was no sound of billiard balls. We went into the reading room. The Western magazines were neatly displayed. That was all. There was no sign of anyone perusing them. We then entered the room used for *shogi*[39] and card games and sat down. But apart from our own three seats, the other chairs and tables were desolately empty.

'It's too late. There are no Westerners here today, so it's boring,' said Zekō.

The awkwardness of his English was unsurpassed. Such remarks struck me as very strange.[40]

'When you are here in Dairen, do you regularly come to the 'Barbarossa'?' I asked him.

'Well – I've never been here before!' he replied in a casual tone.

When I asked him whether this place bored him to tears when there were no Westerners to be seen or whether, on the contrary, their absence delighted him, he answered:

'I'm the President, you know. I accepted this office on condition that I would not have to be on the premises,' he explained in a nonchalant tone.

I was hardly surprised when I saw the members' nameplates. There were numerous foreign-sounding ones. Kunizawa opened a large register and got me to enter my name in it. Then he turned to Zekō:

'Come here!' he said peremptorily.

'Certainly!' Zekō replied, entering his own name after the words 'Proposed by . . .'.

Kunizawa did the same under the heading 'Seconded by . . .'.[41] I thus became entitled to visit the Club whenever I wished during my stay in Dairen. We all three then went to the bar. Its manager was Chinese. We ordered drinks in a language unrecognizable as English, Chinese, or Japanese. We conversed while consuming an alcoholic beverage with a curious red tint. Slightly tipsy, we went out into the street. The dark sky had become clearer and clearer and we noticed the twinkling of the stars in the firmament, which had acquired an unimaginable depth. Kunizawa took the trouble to see us back to the hotel. When we entered the foyer, the clock facing us struck midnight. Kunizawa, hearing the twelve strokes, wished me good night and promptly departed.

8

In the foyer the next morning, Zekō ordered himself a horse-carriage.

'Do you require a *brougham*?'[42] asked the groom.

'No, I prefer an open carriage,' he instructed him.

From the top of the stone steps where I was standing, I looked at the broad avenue that extended in a straight line from the hotel entrance as far as the Nihonbashi Bridge [see Plate 17]. In Dairen, the sun shone brighter than in Japan. Even though the sun appeared to be a great distance away, its brightness made it seem much closer. As a result, the air seemed more transparent. Everything stood out very clearly: the streets, the trees, the rooftops, the bricks.

Soon I could detect the sound of footsteps. Zekō's carriage had stopped in front of us. We rode across the bridge, swaying lightly in the radiant air. The town stretched away on the other side. As soon as we had crossed, we found ourselves close to the head offices of the Railway Company. Instead of entering the next town, the carriage veered suddenly to the right. If one looked carefully, one could make out a rather impressive obelisk rising from the top of a hill towards the blue sky. It made one think of a white sword brandished straight up towards space.[43] In the background, we could see the top of a wide building, also white, except that the roof had been painted in dull red colours. In front of the building, there was also a pretty little bridge. Looking at this bridge, the tower, and the obelisk, one might notice that they were all three the same colour and were shining resplendently in the brilliant sunlight. I gazed at these three structures from afar and felt an interest in the link between their positions and their shapes. I was struck with admiration at the harmony that the combination exuded. From my seat in the carriage, I asked Zekō what it was, and he explained as follows:

'That's "Electricity Park" over there.[44] Even in Japan, there is nothing like it. There are a large number of entertainment installations, all operated by electricity. Our firm created that park to provide recreation opportunities for the inhabitants of Dairen.'[45]

I was very grateful to him for having brought this park into being. And since he had told me there was nothing like it in Japan, I assumed it would have something quite exceptional to offer.

'You mentioned amusements. What exactly does one do there?'

After I had repeated my question, he said:

'Well, amusement means just what the characters indicate – amusement.'[46]

His reply struck me as rather strange. Continuing my investigation, I learned that the park was to be inaugurated at the end of the month and that, until then, even the President himself did not know what activities might be pursued there.

Meanwhile, the horse-drawn carriage arrived at the spot where the electric railway track ran. Zekō explained to me that the electrified line, just like the amusement park, would come into operation by the end of the month. His company was now hiring drivers and guards, and trial runs were being conducted on this particular line segment in order to train the new personnel. The

Chinese were being taught to recite: 'Do not leave your belongings on the train!' and 'All aboard! The train is ready to depart!' It wasn't at all surprising that the line had been extended so far. But if one examined it carefully, the rails seemed to have been laid differently from the Japanese way. Apparently, they did not adopt the same support mechanisms.

'Do they suffer from a shortage of granite, by any chance?' I asked him.

I immediately got a volley of reproaches.

'It's not that at all!' And then Zekō enlightened me on the new construction methods, explaining how the foundations were prepared and how one could form an entire track from a single bar by securing the rails to one another with a metal coating. His remarks reflected great pride. I could have sworn I was talking to an engineer. People coming from the metropolis are so often treated like country bumpkins. There is no way around it!

'It is a remarkable process! I am full of admiration!' I said.

'I have every confidence in the engineers. I have their instructions carried out to the letter, without introducing any modifications of my own. That's how one gets such good work done,' he said.

Apparently, in the cities, people still nosily mind other people's business.

The carriage reached the top of the hill. The road was not yet finished, and I noticed that I was sprinkled with the yellow Manchurian earth from the toe caps of my shoes to the knees of my trousers. We travelled onwards a little. Then the roadway became firm and resonant, as it had been in front of the hotel. Zekō, appearing to understand this change and to consider it a matter of pride, purposely remained silent.

9[47]

'This over here is unrefined colza oil.[48] Whereas this, in contrast, is refined. They are not only different in colour, but have a slightly different aroma. Smell and examine them for yourself!' said the engineer, himself also sniffing concertedly at the liquids. Could it be because of the special process used to refine it? I do not know. In any case, the fact remains that it is fit for human consumption. And since animal oil is quite expensive abroad, producing colza oil could lead to great practical advantages. First of all, it is very cheap

– it is only a third or a quarter of the price of olive oil. Secondly, as regards its relative effectiveness, colza and olive oil are comparable to each other over the whole world. From both these perspectives, then, colza oil is truly practical. Finally, unlike other vegetable products, it has the virtue of being easily digestible. In fact, it has rapidly become quite popular since it was first discovered to aid digestion in the same way as animal oils do. When I asked whether it could be used for frying *tempura*, the engineer replied: 'Certainly!'

'In the near future, I should be able to eat *tempura* fried in colza oil!' I marvelled as I left the room.

As I departed, I was handed an oblong box.

'It will add to your luggage I'm afraid, but we would like you to have this!'

'Whatever can it be?' I said to myself. In the box were three cakes of soap. I was told they had been made from the same raw colza materials. They did not strike me as being any different from ordinary soaps. I examined them more closely. I was then informed that they had the unusual property of dissolving in salt water. All of sudden, I felt very pleased to own the soaps, and greedily shut the lid.

'What colour do you think you might get if you extracted thread from moth cocoons? Here is a sample of what one obtains, using the traditional methods!' said Zekō.

At these words I took a look. There was no doubt about it – the colour was black.

'But if we place by its side the refined threads resulting from our production methods, you will see that they are white. Also, you will see that there are no visible joins,' he continued.

I asked him whether it had been used for weaving. He said that, unfortunately, this had not yet been done.

I then asked Zekō. 'But if one were to weave this thread, what would one get?'

'You would get something similar to white taffeta,' he said, 'at half the price of silk.'

To weave white taffeta from moth threads and sell it at half the Japanese price, would no doubt make good business sense.

Zekō took out a bottle of Korean saké and, filling our glasses, said: 'Look, this is ordinary! This other, though, is refined,' he added, taking out a further bottle.

I refused his offer, saying that I had already drunk my ration of saké. Even Zekō with his definite predilection for this beverage, did not seem pleased by the prospect of a taste test of Korean alcohol, and I declined his offer, both of ordinary saké and of the superior brand. According to him, when Mr Takamine Jōkichi[49] had called on him, the two of them had engaged in a profound study of the relative merits of Korean saké and whisky. Since whisky could be easily manufactured in this laboratory, Zekō apparently consumed it with particular enjoyment.

Pottery products were also made on the premises. But since this was still at the purely experimental stage, it was impossible to say whether the objects were ordinary or refined.

We left the central laboratory [see Plate 22]. After covering 500 or 600 metres,[50] we alighted from the carriage and walked in the grass. We walked so far and so intently that we lost our way. We left the path and descended into valleys. We ascended hills without the aid of any wooden steps. Perspiring profusely, I noticed that the skin of my face was starting to itch; I also had bad stomach pains. I asked Zekō where we were headed. He replied that he was taking me to the Shagekiba Theatre. Out of consideration for his generosity in taking me there, I put up with my abdominal agony and collapsed into a chair as soon as we reached our destination. Zekō treated me to an animated discourse concerning guns. At all events, I think that was what it was. I did not understand very clearly what he was saying at the time. However, I thought I gathered that his firm had subsidized this one building. Two or three thousand yen, it seemed, had been paid over for the purpose of collecting guns. That is all that my ears registered.

At that moment, two or three dirty-looking Chinese made their appearance, holding pretty birdcages.

'The Chinese are refined people, you know! Even if they are poor, with hardly a rag to put on their backs, they have birdcages dangling from their hands. They wander to the depths of the forest and hang the cages on branches, sit down underneath them and peacefully listen, even with empty stomachs, to the song of their birds. If there are two of them, they will even organize song competitions. Oh, they really are refined, you know!' he proclaimed, repeatedly praising the Chinese to the skies.

I took some Gem from my pocket and swallowed it.[51]

10

I had learned with some surprise that Duke Masaki[52] had been appointed Customs Director in Dairen. I had met him just once, ten years earlier, in Shanghai. At that time, he was the protegé of

Sir Robert Hart[53] and worked in Customs. Masaki had left the university[54] two years before me. Since we both had studied English Literature, there was a certain bond between us, even though we had taken up different professions.

Masaki's real name was Tachibana.[55] He belonged to the Yanigawa Clan,[56] and therefore could only be an eminent samurai. The reason he was not addressed as Mr Tachibana but as 'Duke Masaki' was that at the time we were at the university, there was someone with the same family name, of the same age, and even from the same clan, studying in the same department. They were both also lodging in the same home. For this reason, if they had been known as Tachibana and Mr Tachibana respectively, people might easily have confused them. Because one of them had Masaki as a first name, it became customary to call him Duke Masaki. The other's name was Senzaburo, and people called him 'Sen-san', or Mr Sen. Why one remained a mere 'Mr', while the other was promoted to 'Duke', I do not know. Sen did a tour of Europe, either before or after me – I cannot remember. Unfortunately, he contracted a lung affliction there and died in Hong Kong on the way home. So only Masaki remained alive. We could have stopped calling him Duke Masaki at this point, and started using his family name again, Tachibana, since there was no longer any cause for confusion. However, without anyone's knowing why, 'Duke Masaki' seemed to come more readily to people's lips. It was just like my own habit of saying 'Zekō' and being incapable of using other appellations like 'Nakamura' or 'President'.

'Here it is!' said Zekō.

We got out of the carriage and entered the Customs House. Unfortunately, however, Masaki had already gone home for the day, apparently not feeling very well. We had other plans and did not want to trouble the office staff, so we postponed our visit till a later date and left the Customs House. This time, our carriage stopped right in front of the headquarters of the Manchurian Railways. We ascended a wide stairway, which took us straight to the first floor, and made our way to the left wing of the building. On reaching the back, we turned to the right and immediately found ourselves in the Central Management and Accounts Department. With the exception of one member of the staff, who had been sent to Tokyo, everyone was there, and Zekō introduced me to all his colleagues, one by one. Among them I recognized the face of the younger Tanaka,[57] whom I had met before.

'What was your first impression when you arrived in Dairen?' he asked me.

'Well, when I came ashore from the boat, at first I thought I was looking at the remains of burnt-out buildings,' I said, speaking quite frankly.

'Yes, it's military land, where training is ongoing: one can't build houses on it. It makes the same impression on everyone,' he explained.

I remained seated for a few moments, quietly watching the work in progress. Soon it was midday: 'Let's go and have lunch!'

So saying, Zekō took me to the Company dining-room.

'Right along here!' he said.

I had sat down at the table and already picked up the napkin, when the waiter came over to me.

'That is Mr Kunizawa's. I will bring you another.'

Situated on the first floor of the company building, the dining-room was very spacious. In the evening it was converted into a large dance hall. I was informed that these events were open to all the company's employees; however, there were only about thirty people seated at the same table. Judging from this turnout, were there not certain tacit restrictions on admission? Such was the question I silently asked myself.

I was told that the meals came from the Yamato Hotel. The thirty or so diners at the table had already emptied their plates. With my stomach-ache, however, I wielded my knife and fork in vain, without any particular enthusiasm. My throat felt crammed with meat and vegetables. Young Tanaka, seated opposite me, offered me a pear in the shape of a gourd. But I lacked even the inclination to stretch out my hand.

11

When I met Mr Kawamura, head of the Enquiry Department, we exchanged greetings, and he invited me to take a seat.

'On what subject is it that you wish to inquire?' he asked me courteously.

Since I was far from feeling eager about obtaining any particular information, I found myself rather at a loss to confront this question. When Kawamura had entered the General Management Department a few minutes earlier, Zekō had introduced me to him with these words:

'Perhaps you could explain various things to this chap about our company?'

But now that I, a learned and experienced man, had ended up in the Enquiry Department, I felt highly embarrassed when he asked me in a grave tone to elaborate on the direction of my inquiries.

'Er, well ...,' I began.

I bore him no ill will and had no desire to tease him. From experience, I knew that any joking at that moment was out of the question and would have been taken by him as an insult. For want of a better solution, therefore, I adopted a highly formal attitude and declared:

'I should like to learn about various aspects of the general activities of the Manchurian Railways.'

All that effort, just to say something! Despite my serious countenance, my initial comments clearly did not convey any firm resolution; the haziness and inconsistency of my comments, in fact, would have suited an out-and-out country bumpkin. Today, when I think back on this incident, what strikes me as remarkable is that at the very moment when I was tensing my stomach muscles with all my strength, Kawamura was fooled by my forced external calm. Since I had succeeded in deceiving him, however, I could not very well sink into silence, and yet I wanted to confess my sin. At that moment, to be quite frank, I was suffering from a terrible stomach-ache; my body was racked with a dull pain. But, instead of speaking in animated tones, exerting my energy, and over-flowing vivaciously, I continued the show of calmness, quite contrary to my inner feelings. I was powerless to change the predicament in which I found myself.

At that moment, Kawamura produced five or six thick notebooks. The one at the top of the pile bore the title 'Report of the Company's Operation - Vol.1'; the second was entitled Volume 2; the third was entitled Volume 3; and it goes without saying that the fourth bore the heading Volume 4. Depositing these imposing tomes on the table, he said to me:

'You know what it is in broad outline, don't you?'

'Oh dear, oh dear! It looks difficult and tedious!' I thought. At that moment, with the pain torturing my stomach, the idea of embarking on a study of these thick volumes was unbearable. Before opening them, I devised a subterfuge on the spur of the moment:

'As I have no special knowledge of the subject, it would be useless for me to consult these detailed documents; I should understand nothing of their contents. So could you give a general idea of where you all work and your various spheres of activity? That would be sufficient. Would it be giving you too much trouble to ask you to jot down the locations I ought to visit?'

'Yes, all right!' said Kawamura.

And without any further formalities, he reached for a pen. Meanwhile, a strange-looking little man suddenly made his appearance – I could not make out from where.

'Well, well! Good day, Sir,' he said.

I looked at him and saw it was Matano Yoshiro. Some time ago, one of the characters in my book *I am a Cat*[58] had become very familiar to readers. He was a nobleman called Tatarasampei, who lived in the village of Kuruma[59] in the province of Chikugo.[60] At that time, Matano was working in the Miike collieries there, and although I have no idea of how the mistake arose, there were people who all of a sudden started to put it about that Tatarasampei was none other than Matano Yoshiro. This rumour spread like wildfire. In the end, many people, on meeting Matano, would say,

'Hello, Tatara!'

Matano grew very angry with me and sent me a letter marked 'Personal', requesting the complete elimination of the character called Tatarasampei. Although I could fully sympathize with his difficulty, eliminating the name Tatarasampei wherever it was mentioned would require re-editing all the chapters from the very beginning. I therefore asked Matano whether he would authorize me to publish an announcement in the press, stating briefly and clearly that he was not Tatarasampei. He rejected my proposal. After sending me three or four more complaints, he finally made the following proposal:

'The reason why people wrongly take me for Sampei is that we both live in Kuruma, in the province of Chikugo. It so happens that in Karatsu,[61] in the province of Hizen,[62] there is a well-known spot known as Tatara Beach. I should be glad if you would just alter Sampei's civil status by making him a native of that locality. If you would do that, I should be extremely grateful to you.'

So, faced with such a request, I ended by correcting my text and making Sampei an inhabitant of the town of Karatsu, in the province of Hizen. To this day, if you read *I am a Cat*, it will be apparent to you that I corrected my text throughout, stating that Tatarasampei lived in Karatsu.

I had never expected to run across him here, this pensive man with whom I had a strange connection. He invited me to dinner in his home, and for two or three days guided me about the town from morning till evening. With great kindness, he provided me with numerous pieces of information. The fact that he seemed to have forgotten our disagreement and that we were quickly able to re-establish our former, cordial relations filled me with unexpected happiness. To be quite frank, I had been certain that he was still in Fushun.[63]

Back in the office, Kawamura and Matano drew me a sort of chart in which they entered the locations of all the departments of the Company, as well as other places for me to visit.

12

My stomach pains became more persistent, so I retired to my room and stretched out on a couch. At that moment, I heard the rain lashing against the window with increasing force. 'Well, my colleagues who have gone to the ball must be having a lot of trouble just now!' I said to myself. Still lying down, I took the invitation out of my pocket and looked at it again. The front of the stiff card resembled a postcard. On it was a decoratively-coloured rendition of one of Utamaro's beauties.[64] On the other side, it read 'Nakamura Zekō and his wife take great pleasure in inviting Mr Natsume Kinnosuke. . . .'[65] 'It must take a long time to produce something like this!' I thought admiringly. Gradually, I grew drowsy. I had already started drifting off, when the hotel manager rushed into the room.

'We've just had a telephone call from the President. He asked us to enquire whether you intend going on to the ball this evening.'

'Please reply that I shall not be going!' I requested and promptly fell fast asleep.

When I woke up, it seemed that the rain had stopped sometime earlier. The moon shone forth from a sky so clear and bright that it looked as though it had been polished. I looked through the window at the moon's great splash of colour and almost unconsciously prayed for the success of Zekō's ball.

Later on, I asked him about it, and he told me that after the ball he had burst into the bar of the Club, along with a large number of American officers. The officers were all praising him to the skies for the resounding success of his ball, the magnificence of the reception he had given them, and so forth. Then, under the pressure of events and with an enthusiasm born of desperation, Zekō roared in stentorian tones:

'Gentlemen!'

The assembled company, which up to that moment had been very noisy, immediately became quiet, assuming that the President was about to address them. All of Manchuria, it seemed, had become enveloped in total silence. Zekō certainly should have added something after his 'Gentlemen!'[66] Unfortunately, he could not utter a single English word. All English had been washed out of his brain by plentiful draughts of saké. There was nothing he could do about it, and suddenly switching over to Japanese, he followed up the 'Gentlemen!' with a shout of:

'Let's drink up!'

This phrase 'Gentlemen! Drink up!' was incomprehensible to most of the American officers. However, as soon as he had uttered it, the party of officers cried 'Hooray!' and acclaimed him with one accord.

□

I remember the year 1888. We were a band of friends, seven of us, I believe, who had gone to a cheap hotel. Leading an idle life, we had decided on a two-day outing to the Island of Enoshima.[67] We carried red blankets on our backs and some snacks in our hands. Each one of us had twenty *sen* in his purse.[68] Finally, just at ten o'clock, we reached sight of the island. But no one had the courage to take us across so late at night. Then, just as if we had all agreed on it, we pulled out our blankets, wrapped ourselves up in them, and fell asleep on the sandy beach. I woke up in the middle of the night with rain falling on my face. A dog also appeared and started nibbling at Mamizu Hideo's leggings. Finally, the darkness began to fade. When the colours around us became more distinguishable, we looked at each other's faces and saw that they were covered with sand. When we wiped our eyes, sand scattered. The same thing happened when we cleaned our eyes and scratched our heads. In this sandy state, we crossed the water to Enoshima. The dawn winds began to blow upon the island. The countless trees on the hillside rustled and bent in the wind. At that moment, an idea obviously occurred to Zekō, who was standing close to me and who said:

'What's happening? Look at those trees! They seem terrified!'

It was certainly the first time he had ever seriously used the term 'terrified' to describe trees and grass, and we all nicknamed him 'Terrified' for some time afterwards. Now, once again, Zekō perhaps was thinking that there was nothing inappropriate about this epithet 'Terrified'. From Zekō's point of view, the exclamation 'Gentlemen! Let's drink up!' was just as comprehensible to the officers, as if he had said it in American English. The proof that the message had hit the mark was surely the wholehearted acclamation he received. He was a man who, when drunk, had no inhibition about uttering such remarks.

13

One evening, young Tsuda, who worked in the shipyards at Kawasaki, invited me to join him for dinner. At that very moment, however, my stomach was causing me great pain, so I declined his offer with many apologies. In my room, I drank some broth and went to sleep. The next morning, I woke up certain that I would feel better. I concentrated my attention on my abdomen and probed the afflicted area with my finger to check my condition. There was no getting around it: something was definitely wrong. I felt anxious, since my stomach had been consistently letting me down. However, when I pressed various parts of my abdomen, it produced no particular local reaction. The dull pain only insidiously spread itself everywhere like clouds gradually gathering in the sky. Looking depressed, I descended to the dining-room. After having eaten breakfast, I returned to my room once again. I had entirely abandoned myself to idleness, when Kawamura appeared in the doorway.

'This evening, a member of the Company, who has just been put in charge of "excursions",[69] would like to invite you to the Sempo Restaurant along with two or three others,' he said in deferential tones.

'I am really very sorry!' I said, refusing his offer and explaining the reasons.

'Oh, all right!' replied Kawamura. 'To tell you the truth, the President is too busy at the office himself.'

So saying, he took his leave. As soon as he had gone, Matano walked in unannounced, wearing a suit with a white open-necked shirt. I admired his outfit. We talked for a few moments. Then another visitor was announced. On reading the visiting card I had been handed – 'Hashimoto Sagorō, Professor at the University of Tōhoku' – I yelped.

Together with Hashimoto Sagorō, back in 1884, I had rented the second floor of the Shinfukuji Temple, near Gorakumiza in the Koishikawa district of Tokyo, where we used to prepare our meals together. During that period, we were able to pay our rent, eat beef every other day, and consume high-quality rice for two yen per month, all told. When I say 'eat beef', I mean that we prepared a full pot of soup and then added a few slices of meat, which floated on the surface. Since the meat had to feed seven and could only cost ten sen, there was no alternative. We served rice out of a hot cauldron. It was hard work carrying this enormous receptacle up to the first floor, which was higher than the normal level. While we lived in these lodgings, Hashimoto and I were both cramming to gain admission to prep school.[70] He was better than I was at both Mathematics and English. When the day of the entrance examination arrived, the algebra test was difficult and I did not know where to turn. I got Hashimoto, seated nearby, quietly to give me directions. Thanks to his help, I got through, while this fellow student, who had given me the solution, thoroughly failed the exam. As for me, as soon as I got to the University, I contracted appendicitis. Speaking of which, mashed red beans[71] were sold every evening in front of the temple, and every evening I ate some, as if following a set rule. The clicking of fans indicated that the street stalls were opening. As soon as I heard this sound, I had an irresistible urge to eat bean paste. One could almost have said that the old man who kept the stall bore responsibility for my appendicitis.

After that incident, whenever we hailed Hashimoto, we would always call out: 'Sago, Sago!' In actual fact, he came from a farming family in the region of Okayama.[72] Sago made every effort to pass the second-chance exam. But although he was expected to succeed, he failed once again. Under these circumstances, and considering it pointless to be upset about it, he departed for Hokkaidō[73] and entered an agricultural college. Then he went to Germany. Time continued to pass, and still he did not return. In the end, he stayed in Germany for five or six years. Altogether, the time he spent in that country was twice the period allocated for study abroad, or even longer. I have no idea how he managed to pay his living expenses.

It was surprising that Hashimoto had come here, two or three months before me, to carry out a study of the stock breeding situation in Mongolia, at the request of the Manchurian Railway Company. I met him in Dairen when he was just returning after having completed his investigations. When I saw his face again, I found that he still appeared as intrepid as in the old days. But since establishing these new relations with Mongolia, he was constantly busy. As soon as he had pushed the sliding door aside and entered the room, I could not help asking him:

'Well, you haven't changed, have you? Firm as a rock, eh?'

14

'Yes. I'm the same as ever!' he replied.

Contrary to all expectations, he appeared relaxed and even phlegmatic. In the old days, when his actual admission to prep school or a possible failure were at stake, his demeanour had been anything but tranquil. As before, his nose seemed to curve at the end. This made him look simultaneously jocular and severe. I remembered how often I succumbed to laughter at the sight of that nose.

At that time, a great number of us took up residence in the Kanda quarter of Sarugaku. We stayed at a boarding house called 'Suetomiya'. When I say a great number of us, I mean that our group amounted to about ten. When we were all assembled, we acted like fools. It was considered good form to despise studying. Our calling was to avoid preparing for classes. From one term to another, we just managed to slip by. We were really walking on a tightrope. When we attended an English class, for example, we simply randomly jotted down a few translations without understanding them. In mathematics, it was normal for us to remain standing in front of the blackboard until we felt we could get around doing the problem. I myself, for example, stood there for a whole hour at a time, in a state of complete blockage. Each of us carried an algebra textbook under his arm and went to class saying things like: 'It will give us beri beri!'[74]

We formed a band in which most of the members, the united dunces of the class, sat here and there in the classroom, completely at random. I sat next to Haga Yaichi.[75] After each examination, our grades dropped even further. But in the end, when the critical moment arrived, we just passed by the skin of our teeth. Despite this, we were all bursting with pride. At the sight of people who came out at the top of the list, we exclaimed with a superior air: 'What's the good of getting high grades?' Saying that we had to develop our potential energy, we ate meat to excess and went rowing like mad. On evenings after taking exams, we piled up all the desks in a corner of the verandah. Taxing our ingenuity to find new means of showing that we could avoid studying, we gathered in the living-room, which had become roomier, and organized rambunctious games. A boy named Ōkano had bought a toy cannon somewhere and fired it at the living-room wall. 'Boom, boom!' It made a great many holes. When the results of an exam were posted up on the board, it was such an ordeal to go and look at them by oneself that we went in whole groups at a time. We all gazed fixedly at the mark 60, a very perilous position.[76] Hashimoto was a pensive, petulant boy: having composed a poem once, he showed it to all of us. It was a long composition that neither rhymed nor scanned. This poem contained a verse anxiously disparaging the system in which names were counted from the bottom upwards. Nobody could make head nor tail of what he meant. After having listened to the poem several times, I finally understood that if one began to read the list of successful examinees starting from the top, one could not calculate how they ranked, whereas if one started at the bottom it was much easier. This verse was exactly like a divine prophecy. Listening to these prophecies gave us all cold shivers.

While this was going on, a new situation arose: whether one counted from the top downwards or from the bottom upwards, certain names began to disappear from the class roster. One name was found to be missing, then another. Hashimoto, then Zekō. Then it was me. When I met Zekō in Dairen, the conversation returned to our failure in the exams:

'You, too, old boy, got yourself ploughed! That reassures me!' he said, bouncing with glee.

'It doesn't matter if I failed – there are different kinds of failure, you know. The fact that I took it over again is something perfectly honourable!' I replied.

While Zekō, the present Chief of Police of Port Arthur, and I all miraculously managed to catch up by taking the exam a second time, Sago was the only one who resolved to flee to Hokkaidō. I could never have imagined that the latter, whom we should have dubbed the instigator of exam failure, would have become so affable as the years passed.

'I shall call in at the Company offices this afternoon to tell you about my visit to Mongolia,' he told me.

15

Looking at the little note Mr Kawamura had written, I found only about ten names under the heading 'Entertainment Establishments'. They were either clubs or associations. They included golf clubs and sailing clubs. I noticed that by a few prominent names under 'Sailing Club', the words 'a boat' appeared in brackets. Referring to clubs that had only just opened, this meant that for the moment their entire fleet consisted of a single sailboat. Among the places that it was absolutely vital for me to visit were the Dairen Clinic in the Yamagi-cho quarter, the professional training centre of Kodama-cho, the Omi-cho home, and the Hama-cho power station. Altogether I noted fifteen or sixteen places to visit. It was therefore no surprise when I was told:

'Well, if you don't spend at least a week in Dairen, you won't have time to have even a brief look at the Company's installations.'

In addition to this, Zekō had abruptly pointed out:

'We must go everywhere without fail and without making any distinctions.'

Well, that was by no means easy. He had also started to treat me like an inspector, saying 'Be observant!' and 'If there is anything that attracts your attention, don't fail to tell me!' I felt increasingly oppressed.[77] Looking through the memo in my hand, I said to Matano, who was by my side:

'Well, we'll have a look at a few things! What do you say?'

It was clear somehow that he would be accompanying me and that he had come for the purpose of guiding me and of making me go here, there, and everywhere around Dairen. However, there were no special instructions to this effect from the Company, and it seemed to me that Matano, acting as a special envoy, felt he was neglecting his job. Before I knew where I was, he had asked for a horse-drawn carriage to come to the hotel to fetch us.

I got in with him. The luxurious carriage started on its way. We drove towards North Park, which was said to be very big. After half a dozen rotations of the carriage wheels, however, we had already reached it, and before we knew it, we had crossed it to the other side. He then took me to what was known as the Company's Staff Club. I learned that Nō Theatre declamation teachers earned a hundred and fifty yen per month here. We got back into the carriage and went to take a look, from the outside, at the industrial plant where Suda of Kawasaki Shipyard was employed. We entered the adjacent offices, and I thanked Suda for his hospitality of the previous evening. The offices looked on to the sea. The water in the docks was pale blue. I asked him:

'What tonnage of vessels can these docks accommodate?'

'Vessels of up to 3000 tons can use them,' he replied. 'The dock entrance is about 120 metres wide.'

Looking out of the window at the calm water of the docks, it appeared as if the waves, shaped by the sun high in the sky, were resisting the constraint placed upon them and yearning to float freely. I thought how pleasant it would be to go for a summer swim in these roadsteads paved with large stones.

'And where are we heading now?' I asked Mr Matano.

'Let's go to the electricity works!' he offered.

After the *Tetsureimaru* had docked at Dairen [see Plate 19], the first thing that caught my eye was the long, red silhouette of the power station's chimney, directly reflected in the water [see Plate 20]. The people on the boat informed me that it was the tallest chimney in East Asia. Matano confirmed the truth of this. Apart from that, however, on venturing inside the station, visitors received a most disagreeable impression. In one part of the building, the four walls were composed of bricks piled high, one upon the other. There was a hole in the ceiling, through which one could see the blue sky. Perhaps it would have been a good idea to have built a higher ceiling instead? At all events, standing inside, one quickly became covered with dust and had to listen to a constant, infernal din that made any normal conversation utterly impossible. All one could see above the bricks was the distant blue sky, and this evoked a very strange sensation. In certain spots, the floor seemed to sink under our feet as we walked. In all the dark corners, machines were running at top speed.

'When they are also found in the world of industry, men of letters, owing to their intelligence, are really sublime!' remarked Matano with admiration in his voice.

Just then we made an immediate exit from the building. In sum, I would say of this visit not only that the noise was frightful but also that nothing could be seen there but a terrifying tumult.

Matano was running about in a desperate search for an engineer. 'I say! Is Mr So and So there?'

The engineer apparently had no time to be buttonholed by Matano and remained untraceable.

16

'I went to see a haunted house!' I said.

Tanaka laughingly asked me: 'Mr Natsume, how do you know it's a haunted house?'

Obviously, before I decided to take a look at this haunted residence, which was a model of the Railway Company's employee housing, I had not felt in any way drawn to buildings frequented by ghosts. Nevertheless, when someone on this occasion said to me: 'That's a haunted house!' I entered it without the slightest hesitation. I did not even have time to stop and wonder, seized with doubt, why this building was described in such frightening terms. This supposedly haunted house was whole and yet it looked quite depressing. When I say it was whole, I mean that it was of recent construction. Such an epithet might seem inappropriate, because haunted houses generally are decrepit and old. The walls seemed to be made of brick. The whole facade, however, was painted grey. One got the impression that rays of sunlight never reached inside this house: the building was permeated with a dark, gloomy atmosphere.

I walked through the long corridors on the ground floor, first floor, and second floor a number of times. As I walked, my footsteps made sharp sounds. When I climbed the stairs, the click-click-click was naturally even more distinct. The staircase was made of iron. On each side of the corridor there was nothing but bedrooms – if one could even call them bedrooms, for they were all hermetically sealed. Above the door frame of each was a plate bearing the name of the occupants. The corridor was so dark that when I tried to read the names, my eyes, accustomed to the bright sunlight, were incapable of making anything out clearly. I stopped for a moment and asked Matano:

'Could we not have a look inside one of the rooms?'

He then immediately tapped at the door on his right with his stick. But no reply came; neither 'Yes?' nor 'Come in!' Matano gave a knock on a second door. We encountered nothing but silence. My companion, showing no signs of discomfort, continued on his way, boldly rapping on all the neighbouring doors, 'Rat-tat-tat!' But, to the very end, we met no one. It was like walking through a town that had just been evacuated. When we reached the second floor and found ourselves by a bend in the narrow corridor, we found a woman boiling vegetables in a rice pot. There was a kitchen there. This building must have had one kitchen for every five or six rooms. We asked the woman whether that floor had a running water supply.

'No, you have to draw the water downstairs and bring it up,' she replied.

'Where are the lavatories in this dark place, and how many are there?' I wondered. I inadvertently forgot to ask the woman, as I walked in front of her, about to pass by her.

'That's not the way out!' she informed me.

It was completely dark!

From what Tanaka told me, this building had served as a hospital during the Russo-Japanese War. As the battle became more violent, the numbers of wounded increased. Not only were the patients who were brought there unable to receive adequate care, but numerous soldiers were fated to die without receiving any medical attention whatsoever. The whole of Dairen resounded at that time with cries of resentment and hatred caused by the sight of these soldiers' open, untreated wounds. It was a terrible period.

'From that time on, the whole of this zone became known as 'the haunted quarter'. But I can't tell you whether that's truth or myth!' he added with a laugh.

Still less could I myself vouch for it.

When the management of the Railway Company first established itself in Dairen, this building was no more than a sort of encampment. The premises had been completely laid to waste, and it was impossible for anyone to live there. In addition, the place was even then considered haunted. The burnt-out ruins loomed in heaps like so many skeletons. The people who camped there had declared war, with an energy born of despair, on inclement weather, on penury, and on discomfort. They stayed alive only by burning charcoal in the nearby trains. When they climbed into loading cars with their lit lanterns in order to perform their bodily functions, the lamps would invariably go out; when they wanted to drink from the spout, a few drops of water would first spurt out, but then immediately transform themselves into little sticks of ice. They seem to have lived like explorers.

'Seino, at that time, wore six woolen shirts, one on top of the other.'

'Yes! The cold took him by surprise. He has never since set foot here!'

I became engrossed in the conversation between Zekō and Tanaka and unintentionally forgot all about the haunted house.

17

All the way up to the second floor, I could see nothing but soybeans. Near the window, there was a thin strip of bare floor just wide enough for a man to pass through. I gingerly made my way past, squeezing between the soybeans and the wall and looking all around me. I knew that if I were not careful, I would crush the beans with my heels. I was also afraid that the sound of my steps would be heard through the ceiling of the first floor. The soybeans undulated beneath my feet like little knolls of sand. When I viewed the whole room from end to end, I thought of a long range of soy mountains. Three holes, each shaped like the edge of a well, had been made right in the middle. The soybeans trickled down continuously through these holes and, as it was later explained to me, were uniformly crushed. From time to time a heavy object would fall and make a loud thud; in a corner of the second storey, a little hillock would then appear. Some coolies had come up from the floor below, carrying sacks of soybeans on their backs, and after having chosen a spot, dumped the contents of their sacks. Then a suffocating cloud of dust would arise. Innumerable seeds, together with the dust lodged between them, were dancing in the air.

The coolies worked well. They were tractable, had strong physiques, and put energy into their tasks. Watching them at their work was thus a source of pleasure: they made the sack of soy that each bore on his back seem no heavier than a straw bag filled with rice. With tremendous strength, they brought up their loads from the far reaches of the lower floors and discharged them on the second floor. As soon as one of them had finished, another came up and took his place. There was no doubt that quite a number had been allocated to this task of bringing up sacks of soy. Judging from the frequency with which they arrived, their attitude, the time they took to complete their task, and the distance between them, one could have said they were all identical. They arrived by walking over long thick planks inclined at an angle. A kind of scaffolding, reminiscent of those used by builders, had been constructed to enable them to reach the second floor. As one coolie was coming up one plank, a second coolie went down the other. Even though the coolies coming up and the coolies going down saw one another, they hardly exchanged a single word. They were as silent as people who had lost their tongues. From morning till evening, without pause, they ascended to the second floor and then descended again, bearing heavy bags of soybeans on their shoulders. In their silence, fixed gestures, perseverance, and energy, they resembled shadows guided by Fate. As an erect flesh-and-blood observer, I found that after a time spent watching them, strange thoughts came to my mind.

As soon as the beans arrived from the second floor, they were collected in a big linen sheet and immediately conveyed and poured into a pan to be steamed. This was actually a very rapid process. It seemed to me that as soon as they had been poured into the receptacle, they were immediately removed from it. They were taken out of the pan by means of a sheet held by its four corners above the floor, causing a cloud of steam to rise. Through the mist, one could see the coolies, their perspiring bodies glowing like red copper, labouring valiantly. Looking at the physique of these naked men, I suddenly remembered the book entitled *The History of the*

Chinese Armies.[78] In olden times, the brave warriors who humiliated the vanquished by forcing them to crawl between their legs must have looked exactly like this group of coolies. They had powerful torsos and muscles, as well as footwear made of pieces of raw cowhide sewn together. They lined candle rush around the boiled soy to form a round frame. When the height had reached about sixty centimetres, the coolies went inside, with their shoes on, and energetically crushed the soy. They then pushed a spiral stick into the paste and churned it by twisting the stick round and round. The oil, pressed out by this means, immediately oozed in great glutinous drops into a channel constructed at floor level. By the end, there was nothing left but the soy residue. The entire process had taken a mere two to three minutes.

This oil was sucked up with a pump and discharged into a wide square iron vat measuring about three by three metres. In this vat, the oil slowly accumulated. When I went up to the first floor, I saw three or four of these vats and felt apprehensive when I noticed how deep they were.

'Doesn't it sometimes happen that a man falls in and drowns?' I asked my guide.

The latter, looking at me impassively, replied: 'It's very rare, you know, for anyone to fall in.'

Why should I worry, then, about someone falling into a vat?[79]

'The coolies really work well, don't they? And at the same time how calmly!' I exclaimed, emerging from the plant, full of admiration.

'Yes, the Japanese are incapable of copying them. The coolies spend five or six sen a day on food. Where do they get their energy? That is what I can't understand,' my guide added with a stupefied air.

18

Matano kindly suggested: '*Sensei*, why don't you come and stay in my house? I have a spare room measuring eight *tatami* mats. I have bedding available, and you'll feel freer than in the hotel.'

From what he said, one would have thought that his living room boasted a view, not only of the whole city of Dairen and the near-by sea, but also of the mountain range – the succession of steep heights – that peered across from the other side of the sea [see Plate 17]. It was really, he assured me, a splendid home.

At the beginning, I lent only a casual ear to his boasts.

'Oh really? Really?' was my only reply.

But with such a kind offer, I, curious as always, thought that under the circumstances it might be a worthwhile experience, despite the inconvenience I would cause. I then broached the subject with Zekō.

'You can't go to a place like that!' he told me reproachfully. 'If you don't find it pleasant to stay at the hotel, come to me! I'll give you that room near my study!'

He then showed me a room in the Japanese style, behind his study. However, as I had nothing against European-style hotels, I did not accept his offer.

Zekō was seated cross-legged on a big chair in his study and was nibbling *fugu*[80] and drinking saké. I anxiously marvelled at how his stomach could digest anything so hard. Meanwhile, Zekō asked me, holding out his hand:

'Do you have any Gem? Give me some of it! I have a bit of a stomach-ache too.' He reached out his hand.

Well, fancy consuming something like *fugu* at top speed with a stomach-ache!

'In that case, you'll certainly be cured!' I said.

There was no doubt about it: he was drunk.

I took the remedy out of my pocket and supplied my companion with a dose of it. Two or three days earlier, Zekō and I had taken a horse-drawn carriage and toured the town. I had borrowed twenty sen from Zekō's coachman to purchase this medication. Zekō had been listening and had been a little surprised at the excessive politeness I had shown his coachman.

'Would you be ever so kind, my friend, as to go into that pharmacy and acquire some Gem?' I had said to him.

Such words were out of the ordinary.

'Saying "my friend" to a coachman is over-polite!' Zekō admonished me.

At this moment, he suddenly remembered: 'That reminds me! I never paid back those twenty sen!'

That was the only debt we had incurred with the coachman. As regards the groom, however, we were struck by something unusual about him. In the first place, he was not Japanese. With unconcealed pride, he let his hair hang down in a long, knotted pigtail.[81] He wore yellow breeches and woollen footwear, and held in his hand a fly-swatter shaped like a horse's tail about ninety centimetres long. Riding the horse in front, he had the appearance of a gentleman of distinction. He did not perspire and kept up a good speed. He had long legs and was about six feet tall.

So much for the carriage and the groom. Let us now return to Matano. Having been duly lectured by Zekō, I did not, in the end, move into his home. But I went and called on Matano as a friend. It was certainly an attractive home, situated high on a hill. But it was not a detached house: there were a number of houses forming a row. He lived on the first floor of the last house. Here he had installed his family. When one looked up towards his home from the foot of the hill, one could really have imagined one was approaching an English summer resort. On the outside, the building was protected by a thick Western-style wall.[82] Inside, however, one found a pretty tatami mat that gave off a completely Japanese scent. The scenery was certainly attractive as well. One could see the city of Dairen, the bay, and – across the water – the mountains. Matano's house could have been put to better use. I met Murai there and also Matano's wife. After an excellent meal, which we shared cordially, I returned to the hotel.

19

'What about going to have a look at a Chinese inn?' I proposed.

In the street, Matano immediately opened a door on the left and went in. Three Japanese men were working there side by side, each seated at a desk. Matano addressed one of them, who was wearing a European suit, and struck up a conversation.

'Tell me, my friend, is this an inn?'

'No, nothing of the kind,' retorted the other, getting to his feet.

The situation became rather strange. Matano introduced me to this man, who was dressed in dark blue. He was called Tanimura and had been at a college of commerce. Needless to say, he was not an innkeeper. In this country, he had entered into a partnership with some Chinese businessmen and dealt in soybeans. For business reasons, therefore, he had to meet with suppliers from Inner Manchuria. Local custom precluded their use of an ordinary hotel. When they arrived, they unfailingly lodged with their customers, and continued to reside with them during the entire duration of the transaction. Furthermore, these suppliers did not just come alone or in pairs. That is why Tanimura had converted the rear rooms of the house into a sort of lodging house.

'Could we visit those apartments?' I asked.

'Well, all right, let's go there!' replied Tanimura, leaving his post. He proved a friendly and pleasant guide. I kept close on Tanimura's heels and left the office by the rear door. Matano likewise followed us. At the back, there was a completely square garden. True, it had neither trees, nor flowers, nor a lawn: it was just a piece of ground that had been levelled. On the other side of it, we found a reception room. There was a lowered wooden floor at the entrance.[83] At the back, raised slightly above floor level, was some Japanese bedding that had been unfolded and spread out. On it were seated people who, our guide informed us, were engaged in business discussions. To enable them to take a rest, however, there was also a bag stuffed as a pillow. Was it meant as an elbow rest or as a place to lay one's head? I do not know the answer, and I did not enquire into it any further. While engaged in their business transactions, these people were smoking opium or tobacco. The pipe was quite an apparatus, the tin body filled with water. A pipe gave passage to the smoke, which escaped from the body of the apparatus, passing through the water and rising to the end of the pipe. Anyone not accustomed to smoking by this method would have risked inhaling mouthfuls of water.

'Try a puff!' they suggested to me.

So I tried. It made a noise, and I felt I was imbibing nicotine.

Our companion informed us that the soy suppliers lodged on the first floor. We went to have a look, and I discovered that it had plenty of rooms. In one of them, four men were engaged in a game of chance. The equipment for this game was most elegant. The four players divided between them about fifty or sixty pieces, of a size and thickness reminiscent of the 'tower' or 'jester' in a game of *shogi*, and they played the game by arranging the pieces in front of themselves and exchanging them. Each was a piece of polished bamboo with a thin layer of ivory adhered to the back. Various designs were engraved on the ivory parts. It looked to me as if the player who collected the largest number of pieces with the same design was the winner. The bamboo and the ivory made sharp clicks when they came in contact with each other. I was told that this was a game of chance in which people bet for money. I did not, however, comprehend it at all. Nevertheless, I wanted to have two or three ivory and bamboo pieces myself.[84]

In one room, there were five or six people gathered together, listening to someone playing the flute. We pulled the curtain back and poked our heads through. The flute playing came to an abrupt halt. I thought they would soon start again and therefore remained for another moment in the room. But the flute was no longer to be heard. In the middle of the room, a strange-looking piece of calligraphy was ostentatiously stuck to the wall. Although it was of no particular artistic merit, it seemed to be proclaiming pretentiously: 'See, I am expressing such-and-such a thing for my master!' Matano said something, and the Chinese opposite him replied. From the remarks that passed between them, however, I had the impression that they had not understood each other very clearly at all.

20

If one proceeded straight up the hill after leaving the pier, one would reach the town. But if one did not go straight, but rather bore to the left in the direction of the line of warehouses stretching into the distance, one would reach the house of Mr Aioi after 300 to 400 metres or so. His parlour, situated on the first floor of a Western-style building, was attractively decorated with an old statue of Buddha, a mirror, articles of copper and several pieces of pottery. One glance at this room was enough to show that it belonged to a man of taste. Mr Aioi was employed by the Manchurian Railway Company as wharf manager.

To put things simply, he was in charge of all the dockers who loaded and unloaded the vessels. Before taking up this post, when the Moji workers had gone on strike against the Mitsui management,[85] Mr Aioi had offered to take charge of negotiations. He had so skilfully succeeded in settling the dispute that the Railway Company afterwards offered him a position supervising all the dockers. Mr Aioi certainly had the makings of an administrator. When negotiations had begun with the company concerning his position, he hurriedly returned to Dairen, even though his little child had become seriously ill. A week later he learned of his death. I was told that Aioi had already known, when leaving his home, that he would receive this sad news.

As soon as he arrived, he assembled all the employees, whether dockers or not, whose work was connected with the wharves, formed them into a kind of clan, and had a little village built there. Passing by his house, it was easy to see that all the buildings on either side of the street were under his control. They included a library, a club, a gymnasium, an auditorium, and, needless to say, living quarters for all the personnel.

In the club they were playing billiards. The library contained the complete works of Shakespeare and Robert Palgrave's *Dictionary of Political Economy*.[86] There were also two or three volumes of my own works.

'This room is used as a *dōjo* for judo practice, but it also sometimes serves as a lecture hall.'

Listening to Aioi's explanations, I cast a glance at the interior and thought to myself: 'This *dōjo* is certainly a fine room!' At the back, a stage had been erected, and everything was available either for a *Yose* performance,[87] whenever required, or a lecture.

'You mentioned lectures. What kind of lectures?' I asked.

'Our own people, and sometimes outsiders as well, are asked to deliver lectures,' he replied.

It appeared from what he said that they called upon people from the same district. It would be difficult to get anyone to come here from a distance. I then became wary, because if I were asked 'Please do come along and give us a talk!'[88] I felt it would be impolite to refuse.

'Oh, I see!' I said and quickly passed farther on.

Finally, we found ourselves facing an elongated, single-storey building. Inside, a passage had been made in the middle on similar lines to that of a bazaar. The entrances to these long huts were exactly like those leading to bazaar stalls. Each hut was separated from the next by a single, thin wall. The entire structure covered about a hundred metres. Stepping across the passage, you immediately found yourself at the opposite house. If you went to sleep on a pillow just by the entrance, you were so close to your neighbour that it would be easy to exchange a lighted cigarette. Mr Aioi went ahead of us. When he entered this narrow corridor, the mothers going about their tasks or putting their children to bed politely saluted him. I nevertheless noticed some of them talking among themselves without paying any attention to him.

'Besides all these people living together in this little village, we may well employ ten times or even a hundred times more coolies, and still the crop accumulates so much that a large portion of it dries up.'

According to Mr Aioi's explanations, in periods of abundant harvests, the quantity of material arriving at the wharf averaged 5000 tons a day.

'The result was that the number of tons put into storage last year during the rainy season was 40,000. This year it will reach 150,000 tons.'

In the vicinity of the wharves, soybeans alone were piled over an area stretching 500 metres from north to south and 1400 metres from east to west. This fact alone shows how prosperous this trade had become.

21

'Say! Who was that just now on the telephone?' I asked Hashimoto.

He replied with a vague, 'Oh, er – just someone. . . .'

Growing impatient, I asked the servant: 'Tell me: you don't know the name of the person who just called, do you?'

He just repeated what he had already said: 'They said it was the Town Hall.'

Hashimoto, Zekō and I thought it must be Tomokuma. The fact is that after I had arrived in Port Arthur, I learned that this telephone call was due to the fact that Mr Shirani, the administrative head of the town, was well-disposed towards me.

At Port Arthur, I had an old friend whose name was Tomokuma Satō. He had the important post of Chief of Police. As his name indicated, he was a native of the province of Satsuma.[89] This was also evident from his face and temperament, both of which expressed considerable energy. One could have called him a veritable advertisement for Satsuma. I had made his acquaintance in a squalid school situated in the Surugadi district of Tokyo. [90] Satō and I were attending this school in preparation for the entrance exam for the preparatory college. We thus had a connection stemming back many years. In those days, Satō wore a kimono with short narrow sleeves. He also wore a pair of traditional trousers, or *hakama*, which left his shins exposed. For anybody like me, a native of Tokyo, there was something quite strange in his traditional appearance. One could have sworn he was a warrior of the army of Byatsukō,[91] with a resolution to commit *hara-kiri*. He gave the impression of having come to Tokyo simply in order to take the entrance exam for the university. Needless to say, he came to class shod in *geta* as well.[92] He was, however, not the only one. Everybody wore these. There was no alternative, since we were forbidden to come to school in slippers or barefoot. There was a hole in the floor, and if one were not careful, one could easily fall under the veranda or scratch one's legs. The entrance to the rooms was in a bad state of repair.

The school had been installed in the old reception rooms without any remodelling or reconstruction, so classes simply started where the hall ended. One rainy day, I was in the hall waiting for class to start, when a postal employee in a black oilskin passed through the entrance, wearing a wide and bulbous round hat. I was struck by something very strange: this postman was holding a cast-iron kettle in his hand. He was also barefoot.

Needless to say, he had no socks, nor even straw sandals.[93] Under normal circumstances, on reaching the entrance hall, he should have shouted 'Post!', but instead he strode up silently from the raised entry[94] to the classroom. In other words, my postman turned out to be Satō! I was dumbfounded. But why was he holding a cast iron kettle? So far, I have not had the opportunity to ask him about this.

Satō became a boarder at the school. One day, when he and his fellow students had staged a revolt against the cook because of the inedible meals, he was struck and sustained an injury to his forehead. For some days he wore a white bandage round his head. Viewed from behind, his headband made him look like a very dangerous man.

'I got a beating from the cook,' he told me jokingly.

He really had paid a heavy price. To this day, I can remember his formerly dapper profile.

Satō did not have much hair to begin with. It resembled the baldness of a decrepit old man. It was exactly like an under-nourished prairie, where grass never grew to be shiny green and never amassed in thick, dense patches. To use a Chinese expression, one could say he had his hair cut short. When the wind blew, his hairs bent over one by one. Even when he started at the preparatory college, he did not have much hair. Everybody made fun of him and called him 'winter sparrow'. At that time I did not know what a winter sparrow looked like. But I thought it must look like Satō's head, and I teased him by calling him 'winter sparrow' when we were together.[95] The student who had invented this nickname had become an engineer and is now living in Hokkaidō.

I must be giving you the impression that I am starting where I ought to have ended. But when, on arriving in Port Arthur, I found Satō again after many years of separation, and I looked at his head, I noticed to my astonishment that his hair had grown, looked well groomed and even dense. However, it was no longer black.

'Recently, in legitimate self-defence, I had it cropped like this', he told me.

The next morning, we received a second telephone call from Port Arthur. Hashimoto and I took the train in order to meet an old friend and visit the battlefields of the Russo-Japanese War.[96] While I was getting into the carriage, Zekō asked me to give Tomokuma his kind regards. He apparently had something to do and crossed over the station, accompanied by Kunizawa. They went off on foot in a curious direction. Soon afterwards, something blocked my view and their silhouettes disappeared from sight. For the first time, I noticed the famous colour of Manchuria, the bright yellow colour of sorghum. The train continued on to the vast plain.

22

'Say, when we get to Port Arthur, what about going to a Japanese-style inn? It's been such a long time,' I said to Hashimoto, hoping for his agreement.

'Oh yes! We'll wear *yukata* and live like men of leisure. It's a good idea,' he replied, giving my proposal his approval.

Since he had just returned from Mongolia, it was natural that he would start to give me a lively account of Chinese inns. There was certainly nothing I could have added to his account.

'This inn has a great reputation in the Saihoku region.[97] It far exceeds all other inns south of the Yangze River. Here you see some examples of the notices that cover the walls!' he explained.

He had copied a number of inscriptions into his notebook. In the train [see Plate 15] he read aloud a variety of useless quotations.

The two of us alighted, laughing, on to the Port Arthur platform, picturing a pretty Japanese-style inn in our imaginations. A horse-drawn carriage awaited us by the platform. We were asked for our names.

It was a carriage sent from the Town Hall. When we discovered that the man who had invited us to get in was Watanabe, Secretary of the Town Hall, we felt greatly obliged to him. I turned to Hashimoto again and saw that, as usual, he had his nose turned up and was wearing a Taiwanese Panama, or some such hat, full of dents.

'I say, what are we going to do about the inn?'

'Well, let's do as we planned,' I replied.

We nevertheless could not avoid getting into the carriage.

Generally speaking, whenever I went anywhere with Hashimoto, it became obvious to me that for many years he had always been the problem-solver: he would tell me that something or other would be managed, and I generally left the arrangements to him. This time again, as I expected, he started addressing inquiries to Mr Watanabe.

'We came here hoping to find a Japanese-style inn.'

'There is no Japanese-style inn available. You would do better to go to the Hotel Yamato,' he advised us [see Plate 14].

A few seconds later, the carriage started off in the direction of the new town. After a quarter of an hour, we reached the hotel and were taken up to the second floor. We took two communicating rooms. I took a brush out of my travelling bag and brushed my clothes, which were covered with dust. Then, wishing to have a little rest, I sat down in an easy chair. There was deep silence all around, as if people were watching us and listening. One had the impression that there was not a single guest in the hotel. Outside, too, no inhabitants were to be seen. I went on to the veranda and looked down at the road. Underneath the balustrade, the grass was growing in the cracks between the cobblestones. The blades of grass were about thirty centimetres long. I counted two or three bushy tufts. Although it was broad daylight, the humming of the insects was only faintly audible. The house next door seemed vacant. The gateway and the front entrance, both tightly closed, were covered with ivy. I looked towards the other side of the street and saw opposite me a red brick building larger than the hotel. However, there were only the brick walls: neither a roof nor windows had been added. Pieces of wood that had served as scaffolding were scattered here and there along the unfinished edifice. The scene evoked a strongly melancholic sensation. A few years must have passed since the construction work had come to a halt, and it seemed as though a few years from now, it would still look just the same. My sad impressions applied equally well to the roadway and to the magnificent sky. Resting my hand on the balustrade, I said to Hashimoto, who was just behind me: 'It's sad here, isn't it?'

The harbour of Port Arthur, smooth as a mirror, shone dark green. The surrounding trees were all quite bare of leaves. 'There are only ruins over here,' I thought, returning to my room. A snow-white sheet had been unfolded on the bed; a soft carpet covered the floor. A luxurious armchair had been placed in the room. All the furniture was new and flawlessly matched. There was a stark contrast between the interior and the exterior. I was struck by this contradictory feeling, until it occurred to me that this Yamato Hotel, managed by the Manchurian Railway Company, could certainly not be a profit-making venture [see Plate 14]. Descending to the dining-room, I smelled an abundance of flowers outside the windows. By the time Hashimoto and I had quietly reached the lunch table, I was telling myself that, if an opportunity arose, I should very much like to spend a summer in this place, without a care in the world.

23

When we had first arrived in Port Arthur, I was able to espy – by dint of stretching my head out of the carriage window and straining my neck – a high tower, looking like a cylindrical column, perched on the nearby mountain. It was really very high up the mountain and very tall, so I leaned as far as I could to see it. But because of the narrowness of the window, I could not turn my head far enough to see the top of the tower.

Our vehicle proceeded across the new part of town, and when we arrived at the foot of the tower, I was given the following explanation: 'This is Mount Hakugyoku.[98] And the big tower on it is the Hyōchu Tower.'[99]

Looking carefully, I could see that it was shaped like a lighthouse. Among other things, I was told that it was sixty metres high. We continued, through the old town at the mountain's base and then took a steep, meandering road up the side of the mountain. At the beginning of our ascent, we could see the War Trophy Exhibition Hall off the road to the left. Satō wanted to show us this place first and accordingly there we went.

This 'Exhibition Hall' had originally been a house, located high on the mountain. The complete absence of trees and all other living green plants gave the site an intensely forsaken air. I was told that Lieutenant A, the only one on guard there, had taken part in the war. This subaltern took a great deal of trouble in supplying us with the most minute details of one item after another in the collection of about ten trophies that comprised this exhibition. He also accompanied us to Mount Keikan[100] and, from this elevated spot where nothing could grow, pointed out the distant foothills where fighting had occurred. He gave us detailed accounts of the campaign in which he himself had been involved. At first, when Satō had asked him to take us to the fort, he had said that he could not manage it that day and would not be free until 4 o'clock. However, when we had begun to climb up as he showed us, and when he had begun to show us, using his sword as a whip, the various directions in which the operations had taken place, he neglected his other business. He did not suggest returning until the red Manchurian sun over the mountain had seemed to grow larger and draw nearer to us. 'It's a pity if he has forgotten his appointment,' I thought. When I drew his attention to the passing time, he said apologetically: 'Don't worry – it doesn't matter.'

And then he embarked on more detailed explanations of the

surroundings. His response was strange, to say the least, and I tried to push him a little further, without seeming too indiscreet:

'Generally speaking, what sort of thing is it that you have to see to?'

He replied that his wife was in the hospital.

Although Hashimoto and I were fairly blunt types, we did not have the heart to ask him a question like: 'Well, forgive us for pressing you, but since the occasion presents itself, couldn't you continue to act as our guide for a few more minutes?' Naturally, we could not bring ourselves to utter such words. While we were still high up on the mountain, the long day came to an end. Night fell, and the moment came when we no longer could distinguish faces. When our carriage finally arrived in the old town, the lieutenant took leave of us in front of a brick wall:

'Well, here we are. Goodbye gentlemen!'

He got out of the carriage and quickly passed through the gateway. A brick wall surrounded the hospital. In one of the rooms, the lieutenant's wife was lying in bed.

I am really embarrassed at having forgotten the name of a man who took the trouble to be so helpful to us. I simply cannot bring it to mind. When I asked Satō in a letter to give him my kindest regards, I simply said 'that lieutenant'. To refer to him in this narrative as 'Lieutenant So-and-So' really strikes me as too discourteous. That is why, for want of a better solution, I call him Lieutenant A.

I cannot describe, one by one, all the trophies that he kindly commented upon in the exhibition room; merely mentioning them all, I feel, would occupy more than twenty or thirty pages. Unfortunately, I have completely forgotten most of them anyway.[101] There is, however, one that I remember clearly. It was a shoe that a woman had worn and that had no mate. It was made of light grey satin. None of the other objects – hand grenades, barbed wire, torpedoes, a replica of a cannon – remained as clearly in my mind. On the other hand, I can distinctly recall the exact shade and shape of this shoe whenever I wish to.

After the war, a Russian officer came to Port Arthur with the express purpose of visiting the exhibition and must have been very surprised at the sight of this shoe. He told Lieutenant A that it had been worn by his wife. Had the owner of this elegant, lightly coloured dancing shoe died during the war or was she still alive? This is something that I never found out.

<u>24</u>

Up to that moment, we had been travelling about in Satō's carriage, drawn by white horses. But as soon as the time came to proceed up the mountainside, we were unceremoniously transferred into the muddy carriage that I mentioned earlier. We were told that ordinary carriages could not make it up the mountain. There was no other way. However, the Russians had built an enormous fortress up there and, surprisingly enough, had also built a wide road that enabled horse-drawn carriages to continue up to the top, Lieutenant A explained. At that time, it had been possible to ride to the fort comfortably without damaging one's vehicle. But once the war had ended, a double-track thoroughfare was no longer required and there had thus been no need to keep the mountain road in good repair. What struck us as strange was that, under the current circumstances, it had occasionally been necessary to dig out carriages that had fallen apart on the treacherous mountain road.

Originally, Port Arthur had been dotted with hills and there had been no spots exposing the earth to the burning sun. When the torrential rains beat mercilessly down on to the steep roads, however, landslides started occurring in places where trees were scarce. But the ground that collapsed in this manner was no ordinary ground. It consisted entirely of hard pebbles. The corners of these stones, moreover, were terribly sharp. In some spots, there were jagged edges fifteen to thirty centimetres long that jutted up and blocked the road. Passing over them, the old carriage shook and rattled and seemed to lose control. It was still more dangerous to pass over the riverbeds full of hidden bumps and holes. On the way to Hill 203, we encountered so many stones obstructing the way that that we had to get out of the carriage. Holding my stomach, which was aching badly, I started to walk, perspiring freely. When we descended from Mount Keikan, I noticed that the horse pawed at the ground. Clearly, an accident had occurred. I looked carefully and found that a large pebble had lodged itself in the horse's front left shoe. The stone was quite substantial and protruded from the horse's shoe by three centimetres. The horse therefore limped by about three centimetres when pulling the carriage. When I stretched my neck out the window, I began to worry. 'Getting into a horse carriage is really something that inspires pity!' I said to myself, sympathizing with the animal. Watching the coachman, I noticed that he put aside his whip and got down from the carriage saying something in Chinese. But it seemed that the pebble was very tightly wedged in the shoe. He could not make it budge, however much he knocked it and tugged at it. Then, with a heavy step, he got in again. He turned round to me, in the rear, and gave me a disdainful smile; then he once again cracked his whip. Because the horse was remarkably docile, it actually carried us all the way back to the Yamato Hotel with the stone in its shoe.

Hashimoto and I had reconciled ourselves to being shaken about in this manner. We left the old town. When we saw in the distance the house that we had been told belonged to General Stessel, we found it extremely stylish. Among all the things that A showed us, there was a little house of modest appearance surrounded by a wooden enclosure. This was odd, because it was exactly the same type of ordinary wooden dwelling that one saw in Japan. A explained to us that it was the home of the famous General So-and-So. Unfortunately, however, I have completely forgotten the name of this famous general.[102] It is said that, during the war, he was the first to fall on the field of honour.

'Another of the reasons for his popularity is the fact that he lived modestly,' he told us in a deferential tone, expressing respect for the general.

The famous man's single passion had been war, and he had been apparently indifferent to all else. In contrast, the homes of Russian generals and other dignitaries were generally among the best of their kind. When I called on the governor of the new town, Shirani, I asked him, for example: 'You have a splendid home. Who was the previous occupant?'

'People say it was a colonel,' he replied.

'To live in a house like this and enjoy the sight of such a beautiful landscape is surely sufficient compensation for being away from one's native land,' I remarked.

At these words, Shirani laughed and replied: 'In Japan, it's absolutely impossible to live in a house like this!'

Meanwhile, the carriage had begun to move slowly up a mountain road, leaving the town of Port Arthur far behind. A stopped the carriage when it was halfway up the hill.

'I am going to take a short cut to get there first,' he said. 'I shall be waiting for you at the top.'

With a determined air, he began to climb rapidly up a short cut on the left. Our carriage once more started heavily on its way.

79

25

When we looked down, we saw that the mountainside was not as steep as one might have thought. However, no green vegetation remotely resembling a tree or bush inhibited our view. Not only could one look right down to the foot of the mountain, one could actually see fields stretching more than a league in every direction. The surrounding air was far clearer than in Japan. Owing to the freshness of the hues, even distant scenes seemed nearby. The dominant colour, sorghum yellow, characterized the landscape.

'Down there, ahead of you, you will see something small and white, like a little finger. Well, from that point a tunnel was constructed reaching as far as here,' said A, pointing at a distant spot.

'Since, in this region, stones usually have to be broken to make a hole in the ground, it cannot have been an easy task to dig a tunnel about a hundred metres in length.' A explained to us that when a road was to be dug from a trench to the underground fortification, it would take a whole day and that advancing by forty-five centimetres was a veritable feat.

Looking towards the high mountain peak ahead and the white object preceding it, I mentally calculated the distance that separated them. The result filled me with deep admiration of the perseverance shown by the troops. I asked once more:

'But how far did they dig?'

'Up to that point over there!' he told me, gesturing with his sword.

From what he said, they must have dug constantly from 2 September to 20 October. This was proof of extraordinary perseverance!

'At that time, the enemy were also digging a tunnel down from the fort in order to frustrate our efforts. One day, the Japanese soldiers, while engaged in their excavation, heard the sound of stones being broken nearby, and this told them that the enemy was approaching step by step, from deep down in the darkness,' A explained. 'At that moment, we destroyed the tunnel with explosives.'

The lieutenant was standing on the hill that had collapsed, and he again turned to us. Needless to say, we, too, were up there.

'If one dug under this earth, one would no doubt find a lot of corpses!' I said.

In a corner of the hilltop, some of the earth had been pushed aside, revealing a dark cavity. The roof of this cavern, about twenty centimetres thick, was constructed of cement. We lay down and edged our way into the darkness. We slowly crawled down the stone tunnel into a trench. Looking upwards, I noticed for the first time the strength of the fortifications. After having destroyed the tunnel, if they had not destroyed the remaining sides, they would have been unable to reach the fortress and the attack would have proven very difficult. Furthermore, forcing oneself into a narrow jagged opening and then invading the cemented and fortified cavern step by step showed a tenacity far above that of ordinary mortals. At that moment, the soldiers of the two armies, each in the dark depths of the earth and separated only by an insignificant partition, fought one another while only thirty centimetres apart. I remembered that A explained to us that the demarcation line consisted of piled-up bags of earth.

'If a head showed itself above the partition, it immediately attracted a bullet. So they lay there waiting and firing blindly,' he told us. 'And when anyone grew tired, he lowered his rifle. Then they started to chat across the lines. They asked for alcohol to be brought instantly, if there was any to be had. While they were engaged in collecting dead bodies, they asked for a short pause before resuming the fighting. And, as it all eventually seemed absurd, they discussed the possibility of ending hostilities. They thus talked about various things during the battle,' A told us.

We all three crawled out of the dark passage. We once more found ourselves on the blind hillock. The sun beat down on the bare mountain. Here and there, there were little flowers resembling wild chrysanthemums. Standing erect and very still, bathed by the sun, one could just distinguish the soft hum of insects. We could not tell whether they were among the grass or inside the ruins. Ahead of us, I saw the outline of two Chinese. But as soon as they saw us, they hid in the grass.

'If they run, then it is because they have come to dig for something. They are afraid of being arrested. However, arresting them is no simple matter!' A said with a sardonic laugh.

At the back, we found a neat, single-storey barracks built in the middle of a wide, dry ditch.

'There used to be a bridge there, where one could cross over,' A mentioned.

But now it was impossible to go down there. The back of the building was built into the surrounding mountain and was therefore camouflaged from the outside. The three of us left the ditch from one side and started climbing up the side of the hill. Finally, we reached a spot from which we could see summits in every direction. The forts that had been formerly erected on these heights had all been preserved intact. The lieutenant knew all their names by heart and recited them for us. As for me, I stood there beneath the lofty sky from which we had no shelter, looked round at the countless mountains, and thought that not even touring these forts was an easy undertaking.[103]

26

Two or three days after my arrival in Dairen, Itō, who worked for the *Manchurian Daily*, requested that I deliver a lecture during my stay.

'Oh, certainly, if circumstances permit,' was my reply, which could conveniently be taken either as a refusal or an acceptance, and I promptly left for Port Arthur.

Itō also arrived at the Yamato Hotel a day before we did: 'Oh well,' I thought to myself, 'he's already here. I probably won't be able to avoid delivering that lecture now.' According to Itō, he had already printed a notice in his newspaper, publicizing the fact that I had agreed to give a talk. Listening to him, I suddenly recognized what an embarrassing position I was in. Itō had pressured me to give the lecture, but I felt incapable of it. I sank into an armchair, burdened by this conflict and feeling extremely annoyed. Itō laughed at me mockingly and taunted. 'You'll simply have to give that talk now!'

His remark was pointless. The fact was that even before I arrived at the hotel, a Port Arthur resident named Mr Waki had already asked me for the same thing in the carriage. Since, in this case, it was quite obvious that I would not have enough time to comply during my short stay, I had left his request unanswered. But on returning to Dairen, it would be impossible for me to pretend to be busy. Hashimoto had observed what was passing through my mind and subjected me to various homilies on the subject: 'My dear fellow, when you are asked to give a public lecture, you should always willingly consent. People like you have a duty to speak in public!'

While I was in Dairen, it was because of him that I eventually relented. A little later, I did give two lectures. In one of them, though, I could find nothing to say and got absolutely nowhere. On the very evening of the lecture, I had decided that my topic would be demonstrating the reasons why public appearances are not easy tasks and establishing that they are, in fact, impossible undertakings. I uttered some very strange remarks. I was grateful to Zekō, who attended my lecture, for giving me his opinion: 'You're really unbeatable, my dear fellow! From now on, wherever you go, you may decide whether or not you are going to give a lecture. I authorize you to do so.'

Hashimoto, the man inclined to remonstrances, gave me only a blank stare, however, and went off to amuse himself somewhere. He did not come and hear my talk. Nevertheless, when someone who lived in the Eikō quarter again asked me to give a lecture, he immediately repeated his previous remarks, saying: 'You have been asked to give a lecture, so you ought to comply!'

And so, under such pressure, I removed the bindings from around my painful stomach and went out to perform the task.

'I shall deliver my lecture before you deliver another one of yours to me!' I informed Hashimoto.

As soon as I had finished, I immediately returned to the hotel without listening to what he had to say and bound my stomach again. Seeing what I had done, Hashimoto said detachedly: 'Tell me, was it painful when you were speaking?'

On the other hand, once when I was forced to decline another kind of invitation, he supported me saying: 'This man suffers from a stomach complaint.' I wondered whether perhaps he was only pitiless when it came to public lectures. At Mukden, however, after we had had to travel to remote and elevated places under perilous conditions, I postponed the date of a lecture by one day. Even then, the relentless Hashimoto scolded me: 'When you are asked to give a talk, you must comply!'

In Seoul, we had changed not only the intended arrival and departure dates, but also our hotel, so I had the opportunity of calmly refusing to give a lecture. This was due solely to the fact that, on this particular occasion, Hashimoto was absent.

The most interesting side of this matter was that the man who so exhorted me to lecture himself later contracted a severe stomach affliction immediately after his return to Sapporo[104] and soon suffered violent pains. Consequently, he was forced to reduce his normal schedule of lecturing ten hours per week to one single hour. And once this hour ended, he rushed away to take his tablets.

'It was very bad of me to force you to give lectures during the tour when I knew you were not well. I had no idea of what it was like before going through it myself. I did not understand before I myself started suffering from stomach pains. Under such pain, it really is impossible to give a lecture or to accomplish anything of the kind. At such moments, mounting the platform and demonstrating originality is awe-inspiring!'

He thus began to praise my merits and openly blame himself. What Hashimoto said was certainly true: when one is ill, it is impossible to give a lecture. Yet, if I had been as ill as Hashimoto was suggesting, then I probably would ultimately have declined the offers, despite his constant refrain: 'You simply must go and do it, my dear fellow!'

27

When Mr Shirani invited us to lunch, I met most of the people who worked in the Governor's offices. They all wore khaki uniforms. As soon as the meal was over, we went into another room and chatted. Satō then made a suggestion: 'Tomorrow morning you should go and see Hill 203. I will ask someone to accompany you.'

'That sounds good,' I replied.

'It won't be an expert guide, though!'

Since we were visiting as private tourists, we did not want to call on the services of an official, government-sponsored guide.

'If, as you say, we need a guide, then an ordinary clerk will be just fine for our purposes. It doesn't matter. Let someone who is off duty or who doesn't presently have a position look after us,' I requested.

I disliked troubling him, and it seemed the least we could do to make things easier for him. At that moment, Satō took a visiting card out of his pocket and pencilled something in the margin.

'Here you are. This man will come by at eight o'clock tomorrow morning. Please let him escort you there,' he said.

Having spoken, he took his leave.

At eight o'clock the next morning, the sun shone brightly, lighting up all the surroundings – the sky, the mountains, and the harbour. When we left the carriage and started to climb the mountain on foot, the air was so transparent that it seemed the sunlight had penetrated our bodies through the pores of our skin. On that mountain, devoid of trees as always, there was nothing but sun. The scenes within our sight – to the left and to the right, as well as behind and in front of us – imparted a sense of gaiety. Suddenly, we heard a noise from the midst of these resplendent surroundings. Then something rapidly scurried away.

'It's a quail!' said Ichikawa, acting as our guide.

'Oh, yes!' I said, seeing it for the first time.

Furtively, it passed before us and disappeared into the wide-open sky. I raised my eyes in an attempt to follow its course and saw a great mirror off in the distance.[105]

At that moment, we were approaching the summit. I asked him: 'These regions must have seen a lot of flying bullets as well, I suppose?'

'A lot of soldiers were killed here by bullets fired from their own camp. Actually, it was not so much that the bullets killed them directly, but rather that they struck the mountain, ricocheted against stones and burst into fragments. It is a very steep site, so when attacking the enemy from a distance, it was impossible to force them back immediately: everybody held fast to the places with the flattest surfaces. The bullets fired by our own men then dropped before our eyes. Whenever a cloud of dust rose, we took advantage of the enemy's distraction and crawled up, advancing two to four metres at a time. Stones inevitably got mixed in with the dust and our bodies were covered with wounds,' Ichikawa explained in detail.

While I was occupied with thinking about such precarious combat and the ordeals they must have suffered, even without the threat of being killed by friendly fire, we reached the summit. There we found a granite post shaped like a prism, looking like a milestone. Glancing towards the left past a gentle slope, I noticed that the earth there was light brown as if it had been freshly turned over. What was strange, though, was the blackish colour it had in certain spots.

'It's because they soaked rags in petroleum. They then lit them and threw them up in the air from below,' Ichikawa explained. He then intentionally went down the slope to a ruined mound and climbed onto it. At that moment, looking down at the distant scenes before us, he explained the route the Japanese army had taken when they had rapidly advanced and reached the place where we were standing. He also described the different kinds of terrain – whether mountains, valleys, or just fields. Unfortunately, I have no sense of the directions involved, whether it was from the east or from the west that they came when they arrived at the top of Hill 203. Mountain peaks dominated one corner of this panorama, and in two other areas all that could be seen was the perfectly smooth blue sea. Standing beneath the radiant sky, I looked in the direction Ichikawa was pointing.

The descriptions given by this man, who had personally participated in the invasion of this region, were extremely thorough. According to what he told us, he had not once slept under a roof from June until September. On one occasion, soaked up to the waist in the water that had accumulated in the trench, he had remained motionless for hours. His lips had changed colour and he felt as if he had turned to stone. As for meals, they ate whenever they could, in the moments when the guns were silent, regardless of the time of day. On rainy days, however, the carriage wheels got stuck in the mud, and no matter how much the horses struggled, the food often did not arrive. If this sort of situation happened again now, I felt sure that we would fall seriously ill in less than a week. When I expressed this idea to a doctor, though, he burst out laughing and said: 'You know, individual constitutions can adapt to almost any circumstances. With time, one becomes just like a dog or a cat.'

Ichikawa was now a Chief of Police in Port Arthur.

28

The port tapered to a point, like the gathered top of a cloth sack, and led out towards the open sea. Inside this sack, the surface of the water was as smooth as if oil had been poured over it, wherever we could see. The first sight of its colour filled spectators with a sense of joy. However, the light reflected so brightly from the water that the whole stretch inside the bay seemed to have hardened, leaving me with no desire to go for a sail there. Naturally, any urge to go fishing was equally absent. I was not even eager to see the spot where the Russian warships had sunk.[106] Something smooth and sharp vividly reflected on the pupils of my eyes.

From the first floor of the Yamato Hotel, I contemplated the same serene colour. Whenever I entered or left the foyer, rays of that same brilliant light would strike my eyes. That beautiful, vivid tint blended with the light to produce a splendid sensation. I waited until someone came to accompany us – Satō had said that somebody would show us around the inside of the port – but it was easy for me to sense that this place was devoid of any human presence.

After I had been nudged with the words: 'Well, let's go!' I could no longer avoid visiting this place where, from the moment I arrived in Port Arthur, others had been continuously driving me. There were five of us on the excursion that day, including Tanaka, who had just arrived from Dairen. When we entered the Maritime Affairs Office, a sailor gave each of us a naval salute. It was the first time in my life I had received a military salute. Satō went in first. Just as I was growing certain that we would be boarding a vessel as soon as he returned, he reappeared and said, as I expected: 'Go in, go in!'

We were standing on a stone pier. A motor boat was moored close by. Our feet were pointing towards the sea rather than towards the building.

Ten minutes later, we traded the officers' company for that of Kōno Chusa and immediately boarded a motor boat. It was clear that the naval officers used the services of non-commissioned officers or ordinary seamen for such private occasions. The motor boat took off at top speed in the chosen direction, fully controlled by Mr Kōno. At the harbour entrance, we saw that several vessels were conveying an air supply from their bridges to the divers submerged here and there. The vessels performing this task numbered about ten; they were all bobbing up and down, tossed about by the waves. We, too, began to feel less at ease than before. I never would have thought there would be so much movement at the entrance to such a mirror-smooth bay. As our bodies rose and sank in time with the waves, and as the sun beat down on our heads, I began to feel slightly nauseated. Mr Kōno, who belonged to the armed forces, did not need to pay attention to such things. His commentary continued unabated:

'The pump over there, supplying the air, is an old system, you know. Occasionally, divers get killed.'

'Oh, really?' said Tanaka, listening to him most intently.

According to Kōno, quite a few vessels had foundered in those waters during the Russo-Japanese War. The exact figure, however, was unknown. A good number of them had been deliberately sunk by the Japanese.[107] After the war had ended, several years had already been spent in estimating the number and in examining the wrecks that could not be raised. Our man told us that they even went as far as sending torpedoes and similar weapons of destruction to a depth of three thousand metres in the coastal zone to destroy what could not be salvaged.

'So it's still dangerous even today?' I asked.

'Certainly it's dangerous!' our guide replied.

'Actually, given the circumstances, I suppose that is not surprising,' I thought. I made enquiries about the techniques used for raising the sunken vessels. Our guide explained the process, and the part I remember in detail went as follows. Using about a hundred kilograms of explosives, various parts of the vessel were first destroyed. The remaining segments were then fastened together with six-inch metal cables.[108] Finally, taking advantage of low tide for the preparations and using a ship with a thrust of six-hundred tons, ballasted with water, the vessel was brought to the surface on the rising tide by means of pumps. We waited and watched for quite some time in vain, hoping to see a vessel raised in this manner.

At the entrance to the port, the banks rose up steeply on each side, as if they had been excavated out of the mountains behind them. A fort rose from the summit.

'From up there they lit us up with a search light. It was such an ordeal: one lost all sense of direction!' explained Kōno, directing our attention to a point on the slope.

Very soon the motor boat, which was emitting a stream of smoke in the opposite direction to that in which it was moving, turned round and headed back to the harbour. We made a little detour to reach the spot where, according to our guide, warships had been sunk side by side. Then we returned to the stone pier. On the opposite bank, war booty was piled up. It consisted mostly of a number of buoys and anchors.

'There are about 300,000 yen worth of them,' Kōno told us. At the entrance to the offices, we noticed a stake exactly like those that were driven in under water to block the entrance to the port. Its end formed such a sharp point that it reminded me of a sword.

29

I ordered a bath. After I had made my preparations, I heard from the opposite room the sound of gushing water. I took off my shoes and put on my slippers. When I opened the door, a valet appeared before I had a chance to enter the corridor. He had come to bring me an invitation.

'Wouldn't you like to go and eat *sukiyaki*[109] with Mr Tanaka?'

In our current circumstances, the word *sukiyaki* had strong resonances of home for me. However, to be honest, I did not feel like eating at all.

'*Sukiyaki*, you say. ... Is it being prepared in a family circle in someone's house?' I enquired.

'No, no! It's at a restaurant not far from here.'

Even more than the mention of *sukiyaki*, it was the suggestion of a neighbourhood restaurant that struck me as astonishing. When I looked out of my hotel window during the daytime, I very rarely saw any passers-by. When I went out into the street, I had an unobstructed view along the road as far as the hilltop. Even the houses, on both sides of the street, were few and far between. The homes that I did see were all built in Western style. A third of them had never been finished and were exposed to the weather. Furthermore, another third were finished but uninhabited. It goes

Zekō Nakamura (left), Shintarō Inuzuka (centre), Natsume Sōseki (right).

2

4

5

3

2 Sōseki (left) and his friend
Yasusaburo Yoneyama at Hongo,
Tokyo, 1892.
3. Sōseki (left) in Kumamoto 1900.
4. Sōseki and Kyo Nakane (1894)
pictured in an *Omiai shashin*
(photograph for an arranged
marriage).
5. Sōseki in Kumamoto, 1898.

6

Sōseki in his study 1906.

7

Sōseki in his study 1914.

8

8. Sōseki (left) with his daughter Fudeko, 1910.
9. Sōseki at graduation day (2nd row, 2nd on right), Tokyo Imperial University, 1905.
10. Wedding photograph of Sōseki's wife's (Kyo's) daughter, 1914.
11. Sōseki with his sons Shimroku (left) and Junichi (right), 1914.

10

9

11

12

Kobayashi Kyochika: 'The trembling army of a
Russian general' from the series 'Hurrah for Japan:
One hundred selections, one hundred laughs',
20 September 1904.
Courtesy Metropolitan Museum of Art.

13

Hashimoto Chikanobu: ' Simplified picture of dignitaries dancing',
8 February 1888.

14

Yamato Hotel, Port Arthur.

15

The famous South Manchurian Railway Express.

16

Mukden Station with Yamato Hotel combined.

17

Panorama of Dairen and harbour from the Yamato Hotel.

A street in Mukden 'Capital of Manchuria'.

Dock scene (wharves) at Dairen.

20

Electric light and power plant, Dairen

21

Auditorium for the entertainment of workers of the
Fushun Colliery.

22

In the Central Laboratory, Dairen.

without saying that the final third were occupied. But even these houses showed in their appearance that their occupants were wage earners who relied on their earnings for clothing and subsistence. So, despite the fact that it was called a 'new town', it actually consisted of few dwellings and few signs of life.[110] The thought that somewhere in this quarter, there could be an establishment providing *sukiyaki* created for me the unreal feeling of being in a novel.

Nevertheless, to remedy the fatigue of the day and the discomfort in my stomach, I wanted to follow my quick, hot bath with a peaceful sleep under the lacy mosquito net. So I told the valet: 'Please ask Mr Tanaka to go on ahead without me: I need to take a bath, which may take a little time.'

Whereupon Hashimoto, who was by my side at the time, scolded me in his usual way: 'You mustn't behave like that! You have no right to reply in such terms to such a kind proposal!'

Since such a preamble was likely to be followed by yet another frightful sermon, there was nothing I could do but go. So I told the valet:

'All right, all right! Say I shall be there as soon as I have had my bath. You'll say that, won't you? Do you understand?' I said in sharp tones.

I made straight for the bath.

And so, without even showing my tired face to the others, I left the hotel in their company. The sky was nice and clear. One could make out the distant stars, but there was no moon that evening. The street was immersed in darkness. A member of the hotel staff accompanied us, saying: 'It's dangerous, so I will show you the way!'

Looking outside, I saw that the darkness was impenetrable and everything was completely quiet.

Three of the four women who were there did not speak like Tokyo women, and Tanaka, purposely imitating the Nagoya accent, started imitating them. The ladies complimented him, saying: 'He's really good! He does it perfectly!'

Still, there was no sign of *sukiyaki*. Without drinking saké, I nibbled on appetizers and began to find the time dragging. Even when the *sukiyaki* did finally arrive, the state of my stomach prevented me from enjoying it.

'If anyone asked me what the nicest thing on this earth is – well, I'd say there's nothing better than *sukiyaki*. That's what I think!' said Tanaka.

The evening had been his idea, and he partook of it with zest. Sitting beside him and watching him, one envied his enjoyment of the meal. As for me, since I had nothing else to do, I went to sleep while gazing at the ceiling. A woman then asked me: 'Wouldn't you like to borrow a pillow?'

She moved her knees towards my head and started a conversation: 'Does this pillow suit you?' she asked.

It was quite pleasant, so I made her the following request: 'Please come a little closer!'

I rested my head on her knees and fell asleep. Surprisingly enough, even Hashimoto had apparently noticed that there was no room for any activity and, following my example, stretched out. By his head, Tanaka started to play games with a girl, using *go* pieces[111] and making a great deal of noise. I was so motionless that the young woman who had lent me her knees began to tickle me under the chin, thinking I was asleep.

When the time came to go, the lady who appeared to be the head of the establishment emphatically urged us to stay the night. As soon as we had stepped outside again, we were once more enveloped in darkness. We opted for a silent route, where there was not a soul to be seen, and walked like shadows to the hotel. The heavy *sukiyaki* we just consumed seemed to undulate before our eyes. I really felt as though I was immersed in the atmosphere of a novel.

30

'Wouldn't you like to come and have some quail for breakfast?'

Such was the proposition I received. A vague memory hovered in my mind of a breakfast I had had with Hamaguchi sometime after Cambridge. It was a very rare event: giving a guest a meal when he was leaving on a journey at eleven o'clock in the morning was almost unheard of, so I just had to accept. As for quails, I had only very rarely had the opportunity to eat any. A long time ago, Masaoka Shiki[112] had invited me to Ōmiya Park,[113] sending me a letter specifically telling me, 'There is quail on the menu!'

I believe that was the first time I had ever eaten any, so it struck me as extraordinary when Satō announced that he had ordered a quail breakfast for us, especially for the occasion. He pressed us further: 'Won't you come? There will be nothing to eat but quails!'

Wondering how many quails he would have us eat, I questioned him on the birds' origin: 'It's the Port Arthur speciality. And this is just the season when they appear in shops and in restaurants. It's the ideal time!'

From what he said, it seemed that he had already procured a supply of quail.

I had gone to Shirani's to say goodbye, so by the time I arrived, I saw that Tanaka, at whose suggestion we had eaten the *sukiyaki*, had also arrived. It appeared that he was going to keep us company at our quail feast. Satō saw to the preparation of the tables and was continually leaving and re-entering the room. He was wearing a magnificent pair of traditional trousers in Sendai silk. But at the back, where the two pieces of cardboard were fixed to keep the trousers straight,[114] there was a strange opening – it looked like a clam split in two parts. The backs of the trouser hems were also trailing on the floor. 'Let's be seated!', he announced, taking us into the adjacent room, which was the dining-room. In addition to the Western-style tables, four little individual tables had also been placed there. At last, the quail breakfast arrived.

When I took the cover off the bowl, I found quails inside. The dish was, in fact, called 'the bowl of quails', and you will not be surprised to learn that we ate every last morsel. Additional pieces were served on a dish. These quails seemed to have been roasted and then seasoned with soy sauce. This course, too, I ate with a healthy appetite. As for the third course, I remember that the meat had been slow-cooked with potatoes and some other vegetables. To my great regret, however, I cannot clearly recall the taste. All this was also gradually devoured. Then Satō told us: 'There's more!'

He had the next course served to us. It again, obviously, consisted of quails. But this time, they were prepared in a Western manner: fried. There was a slight similarity in taste with the roasted quails with soy sauce I just mentioned. It seemed to be a very elaborate dish. Before we even began to attack it, seconds were offered.

As you might surmise, the quail meat had been quite plentiful and, without intending to do so, I had eaten far too much. The quantity of bones that I swallowed was alone considerable. Finding, on our return to Dairen, that my stomach pains had multiplied, I confided in Hashimoto:

'Might not the pains have been caused by eating too many quail bones?'

'Yes, that's no doubt the case!' he replied.

When we had finished our meal, we returned to the lounge. Satō then asked me all of a sudden:

'By the way, you'll be able to write something for me, won't you?'

When I had met Zekō in Tokyo, he, too, had requested, with a silly smile: 'Since you work for the newspaper, couldn't you write something for me?' Zekō and Tomokuma[115] were clearly in complete agreement on this point.

'Just write something, even just one article, and that will be perfect!' he said.

Out of nowhere, he produced a strange-looking piece of paper, specially made for calligraphy.[116] Putting it down beside me, he continued the conversation. Then, resuming the attack, he said: 'Couldn't you write something for me?'

'I'm thinking it over!' I replied, by way of an excuse.

'Oh, all right!' he said, and the conversation resumed.

Finally, I dipped the brush into the inkpot and wrote:
The old capital,
Taking our separate ways,
A song of the quails.[117]

As for Satō, no matter what I might have written, he would not have understood it. He took the paper and read: 'Oh, er, yes: the ancient capital, the meeting point of ages . . .'[118]

Our stomachs full of quails, Hashimoto and I returned to the hotel. We settled the bill and hurried to the station. On the platform, I caught sight of the big birdcage. It was full of live quails, dashing about as if they were chicks. There was still a little time left before the departure of the train. Satō went over to the cage and started to bargain. I approached them and heard that the quails cost three or four *sen* each. A station employee came up.

'No problem!' he said. 'The cage can be loaded on to this train. You will be contacted on arrival.'

He thus vouched for its safe transport. Then, leaving the quails on the platform, we all three got on to the train.

31

My stomach was hurting more and more. I nibbled away at Gem pastilles, drank some medicine that came from the Hōtan pharmacy in Tokyo, and took laxatives. I also applied various powders that had been brought to me from the metropolis. Every day, I ate rice and walked about detachedly. Deep down, however, I was saying to myself: 'Heavens, it's really unbearable!' In desperation, I went to visit the hospital in Dairen. I asked the Director, Kasai, who was giving us a tour: 'Can a consultation be arranged for me too?'

Without any sign of irritation at this unexpected patient, he gave my request his kind consideration: 'Will you come along tomorrow morning at 10 o'clock?'

But when the clock struck ten the next morning, I had forgotten all about this appointment and was scouring the countryside as usual, wearing a cap, the blazing sun beating down on me.

'So, when all's said and done, how far do you think you will travel?' Hashimoto asked.

'Well, if I didn't reach Harbin, it would look bad,' I replied.

Hashimoto, for his part, had no idea of his own intentions. Reflecting a moment, I realized that September was the month during which students were already returning to college and when the faculty were about to resume their duties.

'And you, old fellow, what are you going to do from now on?' I asked, eager to retaliate.

'Well, I should quite like to go to Harbin. But the problem, you understand, is that I have been absent from the University since June,' he replied, still unable to come to a decision.

It was only the pressure that I exerted on this man, burdened by his professional conscience, that led him to accompany me in a direction opposite to that in which his duty called. In return, however, as soon as we had returned to Mukden after our journey to Harbin, he received a telegram from Sapporo. While he perused with a bitter smile this telegram that was pressing him to return, I said: 'What does it matter? Tell them you're away on urgent matters!'

Cheerfully, I offered advice where I had nothing at stake.

After Hashimoto had said that we would both go to Northern Manchuria, I left the entire programme to him and passed my time strolling about, staring into thin air. Hashimoto studied the railway timetables, and calculated the distance between the places where we were to overnight. For two or three days, he entered details into his notebook with great energy. He would turn to me, from time to time, with such remarks as: 'Heavens, we won't be able to take the fast train on Tuesday.'

'That's no problem. If we can't take the Tuesday train, let's take the Wednesday one.'

I uttered one stupid remark after another, until Hashimoto became somewhat disconcerted. After enquiring with greater care, I eventually understood that the fast train that stopped in Harbin only ran twice a week and that the bus was also much less frequent than the one between Tokyo and Yokohama. Apparently, there were only two or three per day, altogether. My companion then scolded me: 'When people like you make remarks like that, it's hopeless!'

It certainly was hopeless. And in addition, my hopelessness was not confined to trains. I had equally little understanding of distances. I could remember names like Liao Yang and Mukden, but I knew nothing of where these towns were situated and which was the nearest to us at any given time. Furthermore, I gave no thought to the next stage of the trip, the place where we would spend the night, or the places we might be passing through. At this, too, Hashimoto could only be surprised. I asked him: 'Do we get out at Die Ling?'

'No! We shall not be stopping there,' he snapped.

'Oh, I see!' was all that I could reply.

I had no particular wish to stop at additional places. As a result, Hashimoto actually had a satisfactory travelling companion, and, as for me, I had an exceptional friend.

When the programme was fixed and I suggested it to Zekō, he recommended an itinerary that was quite excessive.

'What do you say to going to Mukden, then from there to Beijing, and then to Shanghai? From Shanghai you could take our company's boat and return to Dairen. Does that appeal to you?'

'If you haven't enough money, I will lend you some.' It was obvious that if the money ran out, I would borrow some from him. But when the funds were more than sufficient, this, too, raised certain problems. I therefore considered the matter with great care in order to be of assistance to him.

Far from it being a problem of lacking money, it was rather adequate time that I lacked. I did not accept this ill-considered plan; however, when I left Mukden and proceeded towards Korea, I noticed that my funds were indeed running low and did ask Zekō for a little money. Needless to say, I had no intention of paying him back and spent it all like water.

When we were about to depart, not only Zekō, of course, but all the Railway Company officials who had been in the area, turned up as a single body to see us off at the station.

'Never in your life, old chap, have you boarded a train such as this,' Zekō told me [see Plate 15].

On board the train, he took us into a little saloon. The train started on its journey. Hashimoto, consulting his timetable, exclaimed: 'Look! To travel in this saloon you not only have to have a first class ticket, but there is also a 25 dollar supplement!'

Yes, that is what it said in the timetable, word for word. The compartment was indeed luxurious. It included individual toilets and a washbasin. I forgot my stomach pains and stretched out comfortably.

32

It was the first time I had ever boarded the sort of narrow-gauge railway carriage that was called a '*toro*'.[119] At the station, when we emerged from the train, I could only see five or six low structures. I felt that I was being dumped there like a common parcel. Finally, I understood when I heard the announcement: 'Next there is a quarter of an hour's journey by *toro*.'

This narrow-gauge line, which had been built earlier by the military, was still used without modification. The grass was growing between the rails. Both edges of the track had similarly been covered over by grass. Looking ahead into the distance, one could make out two metallic lines just piercing the dull, green grass: the thin lines were swallowed up by the natural surroundings. However much I strained my eyes in all directions, I could not detect any houses. The rails had been invaded by sorghum. Beneath the sunlight, the large spiked ears glowed with a red ochre hue as far as one could see into the distance. Hashimoto and I travelled forward with our luggage through this immense field, under the dazzling sunlight, shaken about by the narrow-gauge carriage.

As for the vehicle itself, it would by no means be inaccurate to describe it as a metal wagon, on to which a long robust bench had been attached, the type on which one sits outdoors. Seen from the outside, the wagon gave the impression of travelling smoothly, without any jerks or bumps. But once inside, one was shaken about as if sitting in a fruit tree – so much so that one could feel it in the stomach. The men propelling it were obviously Chinese. They pushed as hard as they could for about fifty metres, then suddenly jumped on to the wagon. Their light yellow pants, smelling of sweat, touched the hem of my jacket and gave me an unpleasant sensation. Then, when they thought the speed of the train had decreased sufficiently, they jumped bare-footed back on to the track and pushed the wagon, using their shoulders, hands, and voices. It felt much better when they were not pushing: altogether, the passengers' entrails were tried severely.

This narrow-gauge wagon seriously aggravated the state of my stomach, which was already in a bad state to begin with. Riding the wagon, I swallowed dose after dose of Gem and fervently wished we would arrive at our destination at the earliest possible moment. The greater the vigour shown by the Chinese, the more severe my ordeal. Then, when they no longer bent their legs to push us along, and rather let them dangle down outside the vehicle, comfort was again restored. Actually, I heard that when the Chinese were drunk and sitting on the wagon, one of them occasionally broke a leg.

The brim of Hashimoto's hat was fluttering in the wind. I lowered the eye-shade of my cap and tried to turn my back towards the sun as far as possible.

After fifteen or twenty disagreeable minutes, the wagon finally came to a stop. Only the left-hand part of the track had been cleared and levelled, offering a stretch of flat ground. A long, single-storey building straddled both sides of the place where we arrived, in the midst of a dark, sandy area, covering about three hundred square metres of the immense reddish brown sorghum field. The colour of the walls, like that of the building, was still fresh. When we entered the hall and headed towards the lounge, we were only four metres from the window. Along the border, a morning glory[120] was growing. But since there were neither bamboo stakes nor a trellis, the tendrils, leaves and flowers of the plant lay there in a tangled heap. Beyond them loomed a cliff, with a vast riverbed beyond it, largely dried up. Only at the very foot of the cliff could we see a thin stream of water.

Hashimoto and I stood there looking at the vista from the window, as if we were in agreement on it. By stretching our necks, we could see that there was a house right beneath us. Only the tiled roof was visible. Here, as in the old-style Chinese dwellings, a corridor gradually opened outwards. I could only guess at the shape of the parts not visible from my position.

'What is that down there?' I asked.

'It's the kitchen and the children's quarters!' I was told.

As for 'children', I guessed that this term probably referred to the young serving girls or *geishas*. There, beneath our eyes, a bridge extended across the river. It seemed solid enough, but was constructed with a row of planks, each less than thirty centimetres wide. The water flowed as if it had no function in the world other than to wash the sand. If one went in up to the ankles, it was easy to ford the river. When I followed Hashimoto over this bridge, carrying a towel, I stopped half-way across to look at what could be seen below. Nothing moved but the sand. The colour of the water was completely invisible. I was told that about forty kilometres farther up this waterway, one could fish for *ayu*.[121] I had eaten fried *ayu* on the train and had thought that it was a very rare Manchurian food. Perhaps coolies came down here from the upper part of the river to sell *ayu*?

33

The wooden slats of our *geta*[122] sank into the ground like bamboo chopsticks. Each time I raised my heel, the sand crumbled away in all directions. Traversing the sandy terrain from the shore onwards made us anxious.

If the ground had not been so cold, I should have preferred to go barefoot. With these *geta* as wide as chopping boards dragging my feet down, every step I took felt like a step backwards, and it was exasperating. I advanced by a distance of about one hundred metres in this gear and took a look inside a little building surrounded by a fence of planks. It was a natural hot spring.[123] There was a large vat much like those used for making saké: it resembled a large tub and had been sunk in the ground up to its rim. The hot water had accumulated inside it, and it was so beautifully clear that one could see the bottom. Without our realizing it, blue foam coloured the water both at the bottom and on the surface. Hashimoto and I impetuously jumped into this tub of hot water. From a distance, we could only see heads above the ground and we could have mistaken them for people buried alive in the sand. Some of the Chinese actually did bury themselves for certain treatments.

It was impossible to estimate the width of the riverbed, since we could not reach the end of the opposite sorghum field. Nevertheless, the flat terrain that met our gaze covered a vast area.

Water was gushing out from every spot on this piece of land, no matter where one wandered. You could take off all your clothes, dig a hollow in the sand with your hand, and then stretch out in it: it cost absolutely nothing. Furthermore, if you fell asleep after covering your belly with sand, you could make yourself a kind of padded garment.[124] If you immersed yourself directly in the sand, the gushing water was very hot. When you filled a basin with the water that burst forth, the colour was extremely pure, but this was deceptive. And if you then plunged in without due care, you could have a humiliating experience. Hashimoto and I tore off our *yukata* and vied with each other in immersing our hairy legs. But, very soon, after exchanging a look, we quickly drew back. When a man has stripped himself completely naked and subsequently loses his reason for remaining so, he finds himself in an embarrassing position and loses face.[125] So after having looked at each other and emitting sardonic little chuckles, we hastened to leave the little vat and made for the public baths about twenty-five metres away. There, with an imperturbable air, we plunged into the water.

When we came out of the bath and were standing in the sand, we looked upstream at the watercourse and saw a wide bend in the river.

At the bend we saw five or six willow trees of an imposing height. There was probably a village in the background. Cows and horses, five or six animals all told, were crossing the water in our direction. They were far off, and the moving bodies still looked small. They were nevertheless clearly distinguishable by their colour. All the animals were brown and were approaching the bottom of the willows. The shepherd was still smaller than his charges. It was most interesting: the whole scene was reminiscent of the subjects of the painters of the Nanga School.[126] There, too, the branches of the tall willows all are ornamented with tapering leaves. Whenever the calm returned to the boughs, it was in a truly Chinese fashion. Even from a distance, these willows looked different from the Japanese kind. In the places where they grew, one could no longer see the water. Chancing to look still further in the distance, we could see an enormous chain of mountains. The folds of these mountains were separated as if they had been cut with a knife, some of them reflecting the whiteness of the accumulated snow. Altogether, the mountain scene appeared jet black. In Chinese, the range is called the Saigai or else the Sangan. There are many names for these mountains, in fact. In Japanese, however, there is not a single name.

'What is this mountain called?' I asked Ōshige, standing near me.

He did not know. Ōshige was the Chinese interpreter and had accompanied Hashimoto on his journey to Mongolia. As soon as I had put this question to him, he disappeared somewhere. After a few minutes, he returned.

'I am told it is the Kōmajōshi range,' he informed us.

He taught me, of course, how to read these characters in Chinese, but I have since completely forgotten.

On returning, I approached the bridge, plodding through the sand, and dangling my wet towel by my side, when a young, barefoot girl came down the slope. The bridge was not even thirty centimetres wide, so I wondered who would have to wait for the other. The girl had not yet reached the bank, so I went on to the bridge without turning back. Walking heavily along the planks so that my *geta* would be heard, I advanced about two metres, when I saw that the woman and I had drawn to exactly the same level. There, instead of coming to a stop as I had expected, she continued along the planks, fluttering along as if dancing, and coming quite close to me. We reached a spot where we were walking on adjoining planks.

'It's dangerous,' I warned her.

The girl, laughing, made a little bow and continued on her way, brushing my shoulder as she passed.

34

In tones that allowed no contradiction, Hashimoto announced: 'Tomorrow we'll pay a visit to a pear orchard!'

'Agreed!' I replied.

Honestly, I was troubled by a persistent anxiety that I would once again be shaken about in a *torokko*. However, this is probably not the reason why I found it difficult to fall asleep. Hashimoto was already snoring. It was like the sound of an engine – not the sound that one would have expected to hear from someone reclining in damask bedding, with a golden screen at his feet.

The next morning the sky was overcast. It was drizzling, in fact. Opening the window and putting my head out, I looked at the colour that the sodden riverbed had acquired and said:

'I think I will forgo the visit to the pear orchard and have a rest instead.'

Hashimoto put on a cape as well as galoshes to protect his shoes. He was well equipped to deal with the situation. Since he was a professor of agronomy, he was particularly anxious to see pears, chestnuts, cows, or oxen. He got ready at twice his usual speed and left in the company of Ōshige. As for me, I just waited, drinking in the view from the window: the mountains, the water, the riverbed, and the sorghum. The level of the river, flowing sluggishly, was the same as the day before – between about sixty and ninety centimetres. However, in the very middle of the watercourse, a bamboo tube had been buried in the sand. I took a good look, stretching out my neck. Addressing the chambermaid, I inquired:

'What is that for?'

'That's something left over from the drilling,' she replied.

Despite being a Manchurian chambermaid, she was familiar with technical terms. 'In the rainy season, the sand is carried downstream by the water and the current runs in the opposite direction from what one would normally expect. That is why a new thermal spa had to be constructed down there,' she explained.

It seemed that since the current changed each time it rained, baths could not be built just anywhere at random. At the present time, water had almost filled the crevices in the ground in front of the window.

Soon the rain tapered off. Boredom took hold of me, and I lay down. About ten minutes later, the chambermaid reappeared: 'Someone has just telephoned from the station.'

I was told that if I now wished to go and see the pear orchard, a narrow-gauge wagon from the station was available. The rain had stopped, and I could no longer maintain the pretext of needing a nap. However, the thought of the *toro* waiting for me was most unwelcome. Looking at the sky, I saw that it was almost wilfully growing clearer. I frowned.

'If I leave now, shall I arrive in time?' I asked the person at the other end of the telephone.

'It's a mechanically driven narrow-gauge vehicle, so it goes just about as fast as a train,' I was told.

Naturally, I was anxious about the effect of the ride on my stomach, and this caused me to feel rather depressed. But, in order to see what it was like, I wanted to spend a few days in this mechanically propelled *torokko* that ran as fast as a train. I started getting ready as quickly as possible, when three or four hotel guests who were waiting in an adjacent room said that they, too, had to catch the 11 o'clock train to Dairen and got ready to depart. The chambermaid, who was accompanying them, likewise made her preparations. There were thus quite a few of us. Then I saw the woman whom I had met on the bridge the day before. We sat back to back in the same wagon. Being in this position, we did not chat. Neither could I see her face clearly. I could only hear her talking quite distinctly. She was speaking in Chinese, so, needless to say, I could not understand what she was saying. She was vociferously scolding the coolies. Her vehemence amazed me. I would never have believed it of the woman who, the previous day, had smilingly given me a respectful bow and nervously passed close by my side. The evening before our departure, this woman introduced herself to us for the first time. In the light of the electric lamp, she appeared quite pale under her make-up. As usual, however, she did not utter a word.

After an uncomfortable quarter of an hour, the narrow-gauge wagon reached the station. The hotel guests immediately boarded the train, which moved off in the direction of Dairen. All the women returned to the hot spring. I was left behind by myself to wander round the platforms of the station, but saw no indication of the mechanically propelled *toro* of which I had been told. An employee came over to me and told me that the wagon had just left the Pine Mountain, Song Shan.[127] The place was ahead of me in the distance. Leaning on a railing, I searched along the track that stretched over the flat ground into the distance, as far as the eye could see, but I saw not the slightest sign of the arriving *torokko*.

35

A man in Western-style clothing appeared. I did not know whether he was someone who worked at the inn or at the station. Guided by him, we entered the village, where the ground was completely sand-covered. The sand, in fact, seemed to be about thirty centimetres deep. A woman was standing in front of an adobe door, but ran away as soon as she saw us. I noticed the long pipe that she was holding in her hand. A dog behind the door barked without stopping. Soon, we left the village behind us and reached Pine Mountain, or Song Shan. The name was rather exaggerated, though. In actual fact, the place looked more like Asukayama Hill[128] in Tokyo would have looked if it had been enlarged and planted with pines; one felt one was walking through a delightful garden, free of artificial hillocks. The pines, young trees – about thirty or forty years old – stood on the lawn in a straight row. It would be most pleasant to come here in the early springtime for a picnic. In Manchuria, however, such spots were very rare. Pressing my stomach, which was hurting, I finally reached the top of the hill. Up there, I found a little temple reserved for homage to one's ancestors. Going up to the front of the edifice, I started to read the Chinese maxims.[129] All of a sudden, I noticed the sound of weaving shuttles. There was somebody there – perhaps the guardian of the temple. Bending over, I entered the building through an opening in the white wall. I crossed the dark hall with its hard-packed surface and examined the farthest corners of the house, until I noticed an elderly man with a sparse white beard. Seated at a loom near the window, he sent the shuttle back and forth without pause. He was weaving a big, coarse cloth. Our guide said two or three words to him in Chinese. The old man paused in his work and replied in a calm, firm voice. 'He says he is seventy years old,' said our guide, translating his words for us.

'He's all by himself here; how does he manage for his meals?' I asked, putting my guide to the trouble of translating again.

'He says he eats what they bring him from the house down below.' The guide explained to us that the 'house down below' was the home of the owner of the pear orchard.

Soon afterwards, we descended the hill again and started making our way towards the orchard, when our guide suggested: 'It's difficult to go in through the entrance, so what do you say to climbing the bank?'

I immediately agreed, and we hurried down the slope towards an adobe wall built in a semicircle opposite us. My stomach was giving me a great deal of pain. We hunched down to pass beneath the trees, and after covering about forty metres, came upon Hashimoto and the others, sitting on stools and eating pears. The stationmaster was also present with his gold-striped sleeves. I joined the group and ate a pear – and then another pear. When my stomach had something to absorb, I had an hour's respite from the pain. We then toured the orchard. The pears were bright red, just like apples. In terms of size, though, they were not even half as big as Japanese pears. However, despite their small size, they grew close together in large clusters, causing tree branches to bend under their weight. It was an astonishing sight. While we were there, the owner of the orchard gave a servant instructions to gather the best pears into a basket and offer them to everybody. The proprietor was a man of imposing physical stature. He was Chinese and gave the impression of having a very phlegmatic temperament. According to our guide, he was a wealthy man with a fortune of twenty million yen. But what he told us was probably untrue. Our host smoked American cigarettes with high nicotine content.

When we had eaten our fill of pears, Hashimoto instructed the interpreter Ōshige to address him as follows: 'We are most grateful to our host for his kind attention to us and should now like to take leave of him after purchasing, by way of thanks, thirty *sen* of pears.'

When Ōshige translated his words with a serious face, the owner burst out laughing.

'If it's thirty sen worth you want, you can have them as a gift. Take them,' he said, and Ōshige translated.

Hashimoto did not offer to change the thirty sen to thirty yen, nor did he say whether or not he would take the fruit. Back at the inn, the chambermaid told me that she had gone to visit the pear orchard with a guest and that she had bought seven yen of pears as a present. Hashimoto, still with an impervious look on his face, said: 'Well, yes, I thought I would go to the pear orchard and buy thirty sen worth of pears, but I was told that at that price, I might as well get them free.'

36

The wall looked as if it had been built with the aid of a trowel. But it was only ordinary mud that had been dried in the heat of the sun. It touched the ground at right angles, so it did not give the impression of being made of mud: it was exactly like a proper wall. A number of perfectly square openings had been made in the upper part, as in a Western fortified castle, making it look just like a normal tower. But what most attracted my attention, however, were the red flags I could see through the holes. There were as many flags as there were holes, and there were so many that they made the edifice come alive. When I saw this sight for the first time, I assumed that it was probably something that some young people had rigged up for fun on the day of a village festival. I learned, however, that the owner of the pear orchard had had these towers specially built on the four corners of his property in preparation for its defence against an attack by mounted Manchurian bandits.

I was half-surprised and half-amused, but I was in no way better able to understand why a red flag had been put up inside each opening, all the way round the back of the building and reaching up one level after another. I noticed that each flag indicated the presence of a corresponding gun. They were ancient, rusting guns fit for a museum. They had been stacked in a safe place against the wall, and there was no risk of a gun going off, even if it were loaded. Needless to say, the flags had been hung with great care, in such a way that they could be clearly seen from the outside through the holes made in the wall. The sentries all had dirty faces and spent their time loafing in the back rooms. They were guards who had been hired especially for defence against attacks by mounted bandits. Actually, they were coolies who were paid thirty to forty sen a day.

I came down from the tower, and before passing through the gateway, asked the interpreter to enquire whether it was possible to have a look inside the house. Without replying, the proprietor shook his head in refusal. The interpreter explained to us that the quarters where the women lived could not be visited.

'Would you like to see the guestroom instead?' asked the master of the house.

He appointed a clerk to accompany us.

What he called the 'guestroom' actually amounted to a separate building on the opposite side of the road. First of all, we passed a tall willow whose tapering leaves stretched upwards. Then passing through the door of the long building, I saw a grey mule tethered to the branch of the tree. As soon as I caught sight of this animal, I was reminded of *The Tale of the Three Kingdoms*.[130] The mule was somewhat similar to the horse ridden by Gentoku. It was the first time I had seen a mule since my arrival in Manchuria. Its paunchy belly and diminutive size gave an impression of roundness and vigour. It looked like a good animal without a scrap of malice. I listened at length to Hashimoto's comments on mules; however, when he started explaining the difference between a he-mule and a she-mule, it simply confused my naïve mind and I gazed in silence at the bare silhouette of the unsaddled animal. With its head held down, it grazed ceaselessly on the short grass.

After passing through the entrance, we found the guestroom that the proprietor had mentioned just ahead of us. What we saw as we first arrived, after pushing open the double door, was like a Buddhist Temple. The interior was filthy.

'When people are invited, doesn't the place get cleaned?' I asked.

'Oh, yes!' was the reply.

After having taken leave of the proprietor, we once more passed through Pine Mountain, where I saw cows roaming freely among the trees. The stationmaster picked some mushrooms along the way. Ordinarily, they are most difficult to find, but he had known exactly where to look. Just for fun, Hashimoto and I started to look for some, but without any success. Coming down from the top of the hill, I remarked to Hashimoto: 'Travelling through Manchuria by rail, one gets the impression that the land is completely infertile. But when one climbs up to a spot like this, it seems like immensely fertile territory, doesn't it?'

Apparently, Hashimoto did not share my opinion, for he made no precise reply. When I spoke of immensely fertile territory, my choice of words was actually due to the rich tones that the earth had assumed. Viewing the panorama from the top of the hill, under the bright sun that hung high over the horizon, one could see brown and yellow tones separating into bright streaks and melding together again into ornamental designs. The hovering mists then blurred the colours. Continuing up into the clouds, they covered the entire plain. Manchuria was indeed a vast land.

After we had returned to the inn, the proprietress made soup with the mushrooms that the stationmaster had found and served it to us for dinner. While we ate it, we talked of the pear orchard, the horse-borne brigades, the mud towers, and the red flags, and I fell fast asleep.

37

The proprietress came to see me in my room, where I was preparing for my departure. She brought a notebook with her.

'Could you write something in it?' she asked.

She was a rather stout woman. In fact, she appeared to be twice my weight. At first I did not know her position, and was rather surprised, on learning that she was the proprietress, to find that she was not an ordinary chambermaid. Her affable and cheerful manner suited her ample build. I wondered how she had managed to get crafty chambermaids to follow her instructions. Putting the register down in front of her, she rested her hands on her knees as a sign of deference, and said:

'Please write!'

Each of her knees was about eight inches wide.

Opening the book, I saw that H, a doctor of forestry, had painted the words: 'The landscape of water and mountains calls our Motherland to mind.' Then there was a mention of a commander So-and-So of the regiment stationed at N. It was not quite clear whether it was a hotel register or an autograph album. On the third page, something had to be written without delay in commemoration of our visit. As soon he saw the volume, Hashimoto looked away with an air of indifference. I felt obliged to write something, and I was about to do so, when I asked her: 'Could we do this another time?'

'Don't say that! Please do write something for me now!' she repeated twice, bowing very low.

It had been obvious from the outset that I did not want to fool her. But being pressed with such urgency, I felt I would be unable to achieve any calligraphic elegance. So, overcome by a feeling of embarrassment and humiliation, I really no longer knew what to do. Laughing, Hashimoto declared: 'This man doesn't lie. So don't worry! He will write something for you.'

While continuing to chat, I had to hit upon some subject that had the makings of a *haiku*.[131]

I am confessing all this because I feel that many of my readers will take pity on me. When one is travelling, being appealed to for poor-quality compositions is very tiresome. It is true that, in a feverish bout of *haiku* composition, I might be known to resort to scribbling on wooden columns embedded in the walls. However, on days when sources of inspiration are completely absent, if I am handed a special card like a *tanzaku*[132] on which to commemorate something, this pressure troubles me far more than having to repay a loan at the end of the year!

When the moment came to leave Dairen, when I had stuffed my leather case full to capacity, secured my luggage straps, and risen to my feet saying 'There, that's done!', I suddenly noticed at the bottom of the dressing table mirror an oblong packet wrapped in paper. Finding this a bit odd, I undid the packet and examined its contents. They consisted of several *tanzaku*, used for commemoration of special events. Probably someone had come to see me, intending to get me to compose a *haiku* for him. Unfortunately, I had been absent. So he had intentionally left these cards, intending to return and ask me for this favour. I took the packet from the dressing-table, stuffed it into my travelling bag, and left the hotel. To this day, I do not know to whom the *tanzaku* belonged. There were five or six of them, of very high quality, shaped like clouds. When I arrived in Korea, I used these cards whenever anyone urged me to write something. I do not have a single one left. At an inn in Zhang Zhun, the proprietress once again approached me. Using refined words, she told me she was a native of the coastal region. She pulled out two bound notebooks, reserved for the purpose, and asked me: 'Can you write the same thing for me in both books?'

When I asked her whether it was really necessary to write in both, she replied in the affirmative. The reason was as follows: when she was apart from her husband, each of them would be able to take a copy. While recording this episode, I cannot avoid also recounting how somebody at a banquet in Korea went as far as to present me with a piece of white satin on which I was asked to write something that I would have to mention in my talk. But enough on that subject! Let us leave it and revert to the previous matter. Let me now relate the end of the story about the stout proprietress. Being forced to write something was troublesome to me, as I have said. In order to arrive in time to catch the train, I finally made up some lines in my head. Then, giving it the heading 'At Xiong Yue Zheng', I wrote:

> *Millet far and wide,*
> *People crossing the river,*
> *Men take the waters,*

and heaved a sigh of relief. Then, without having time to listen to any thanks from the proprietress, I hurriedly mounted the narrow-gauge wagon. Willow trunks were used as telegraph poles. Without anyone's having noticed it, the trees had sprouted numerous roots in the ground. I was surprised to notice green leaves showing through alongside the wires. This, too, could provide a subject for good verses, I thought.

38

When I looked out the train window, I saw that the sorghum had disappeared without my noticing it. Before, I could always see yellow rooftops here and there in the distance. But these scenes likewise had vanished. The yellow rooftops had been a very attractive sight.

'It's because they lay corn cobs out on the roofs to dry,' Hashimoto explained.

'Oh, I see.'

It was just as I had supposed. Regardless of the corn, I found that their colour harmonized perfectly with my thoughts. In Korea, they leave paprika on the roof to dry in the same way. Under the autumn sky, the lone houses we could glimpse through the pine trees seemed to be on fire, owing to the red colour. But even at the very first glance, I saw that this was due to red peppers. In Manchuria, it seemed to me that the yellow tint broke the monotony of the immense steppes. Perhaps it was due to the distance, but neither these roofs nor the sorghum seemed to throw any shadow. All that could be seen was the surface of the ground. And on it, the grass stretched endlessly into the distance, like dark red brambles. At first I thought it was a kind of knotgrass. I asked Hashimoto. He immediately got on his high horse: 'That isn't knotgrass!' he snapped. 'Those are marine plants.'

It was all very interesting. When screwing up my eyes and looking towards the steppes, I thought I noticed a dull light on the horizon where it was beginning to get dark.

'Is that the coast?' I asked Hashimoto.

At that moment, night was falling. A certain tint started emerging at that moment. A light mist already covered the part of the steppes, and the red grass stretched away into the distance. Focusing attention on what was close at hand and carefully studying the ground, one could tell that it was not dry. Walking over it, we quickly noticed that it was so swollen with moisture, in fact, that the water seemed to soak right through the soles of our shoes. Hashimoto said: 'Because of the saline content of the soil, no grains can be sown here.'

'There are no pigs either, are there?' I asked Hashimoto once again.

The first time I saw Manchurian pigs from the train, I thought I had really come upon an incredible animal. I was seized by such curiosity that I asked quite seriously: 'What is that strange black animal?'

From that moment onwards, the impression that the Manchurian pig was a strange animal never left me. I never lost my enthusiasm for this wondrous beast found here and there on uncultivated marshy land, where there was nothing but this short, slightly dark grass that could have been taken for moss. However, night was fully upon us before we encountered one of these prodigies. The contours of this red grass, which I found unbearable to look at, melted into the uniform darkness of night. Then, like a vestige of the setting sun, a clear patch of sky appeared to the north. Under this light cloud, I noticed something amazingly black. It seemed to be the profile of the lofty ramparts of a castle, blocking out the view of the sky, and continuing for a long distance. At the sight of these high shapes, the illusion took hold of me that we were passing close to ruins, perhaps the Great Wall of China. At that moment, I caught sight of someone up there walking along the top of the wall. 'Well, well!' I said to myself. Then I saw another person walking along the wall. 'How very strange!' I thought. Without even blinking, I stared fixedly at the top of this rampart and once again saw a figure proceeding along it.

Whatever I might have imagined, there really were people coming and going up there. Needless to say, since it was night, I was unable to make out these men's faces or apparel. But there was no doubt that black silhouettes appeared regularly on the ramparts and then rapidly disappeared, with the relatively clear sky as a backdrop. This interested me all the more since I had had no time to ask Hashimoto for his opinion: I intently observed the goings and comings of these black beings before my eyes. At the same time, the train travelling towards the ramparts soon came into view. When it reached a certain distance from the wall, I suddenly burst out laughing. The fact is that what I had hitherto taken for a crowd of human beings was suddenly metamorphosed into a line of telegraph poles, where only the tops were visible. And the thing that stretched out over a great distance, looking just like the rampart of a fortress, was nothing more than an immense oblong cloud. The train inexorably reached and passed these telegraph poles one by one. The 'beings' moving up above eventually disappeared.

39

A brick wall rose up on both sides of the narrow alley. Casting a glance at it, I saw that the passage was little used, suggesting a residential quarter.[133] We advanced by some forty metres and passed under a porch situated to the left. I was unprepared for this arrival, of course, so I do not know the name of the house or of its owner. When I think back on it today, there were a number of houses similar to this one, standing one after another along the alley. They all had identical gateways, which, despite their number, all stood open. However, there was nothing that gave us any special urge to enter this house. I did so purely in order to follow our guide, without any other particular purpose. The guide himself had gone there by chance. He was the keeper of an inn called Seirinkan. Formerly, he had travelled the North in the company of Futabatei Shimei and told us how the Russians had ingeniously cheated him.[134]

Passing through the porch, I saw rooms on the right as well as at the end. On the left, too, there appeared to be a room, but a wall blocked our view of it. Consequently, only the passage was roofless. Standing there, I looked at the rooms to the right and felt as though I was in an alleyway, viewing the little shops installed inside the Sensōji Temple.[135] The shops, in this instance, were little, low-lying rooms. A curtain had been hung across the entrance to the first, so one could not clearly see what was going on inside. When I started to examine the second, I was seized with astonishment. Behind a room with a hard-packed floor, measuring at least four square metres, there were three young girls. The ceiling was so low that they had to remain seated. There was a wooden beam[136] – the kind placed at the entrance to a Japanese house leading towards the room carpeted with *tatami* mats. The girls were neither sitting upright nor lying right down. They were leaning against one another and completely covered the rear wall as if they were supporting it. Their kimonos were juxtaposed without leaving any gaps. The soft material was gracefully pressed, and looking at them, one could have thought, albeit with a little exaggeration, that they all had clothed themselves in one large kimono. Under the plentiful material, little satin shoes peeped forth.

Their faces presented an appearance similar to their bodies. The girls on the left and right had relatively ordinary faces. The one in the middle, however, was exceptionally pretty. Her eyebrows stood out against her white face. Her eyes, too, were bright. The curve from her cheeks down to her jaw was as sweet as a spring day. Despite my astonishment, I allowed myself to be captivated by her charm. The young girl averted her gaze and looked to the sky. As long as we remained in front of them, they did not exchange a single word.

The proprietor of the Seirinkan Inn, apparently not sharing the same interest in this woman, suddenly continued the tour. We entered a room situated at the very back. Here again was a cramped little room without proper flooring. A table had been placed in the centre, where three men were eating a meal. From the plates and rice bowls to the chopsticks and tea bowls, everything was incredibly dirty. The men seated at the table were even dirtier. When I saw them, I wondered whether these were servants devouring their meal in the kitchen. From the adjoining room, we could hear lively music being played. The place where I had seen the beautiful young girl was only six metres away. I had a feeling that these two places somehow did not in the least correspond to each other.

I moved two steps farther away from the Western-style table where the three men were dining and looked through the opening into the next room. There again I was amazed. On the right, a man was sitting and leaning against a wall. A table stood near him. Three women were standing on the left. In front, a little girl of twelve or thirteen stood facing him. At the entrance to the room, a blind man was seated on a stool, positioned a little farther back. This odd group of people were singing songs, accompanied by the squeaks of a little four-stringed guitar. To me, understanding neither the words nor the music, the sound seemed both peculiar and melancholy. The man to the right of the table was holding, in his right hand, an object that resembled a set of divining rods,[137] and from time to time, he drummed on the stool. Holding in his palm two pieces of bamboo resembling *Hatsuhashi* cakes,[138] he brought them together with a clicking sound, in time to the singing. The purpose of this was similar to the use of castanets by Spanish women. But looking at this man's face, one was in no way reminded of old times at the Alhambra. He turned his earth-coloured face towards the little girl's head as if concentrating all his energy on her, and sang in such a frightful voice that it turned my stomach. The child looked fixedly at the man without blinking, accompanying the women with her own shrill voice. I was transfixed by this scene, as though some horrible spectre had put me under a spell. The blind man showed a sombre visage matching his darkened eyes, and incessantly plucked away at his guitar, emitting high, sad, melancholy sounds. A woman standing on the left was watching me. It was an oblique and extremely disagreeable look. In this room, as lacking in light as the close of day, I felt like somebody in a dream. Then, tugging at my guide's sleeve, I hurriedly left the scene.

40

Hashimoto had departed for a distant spot in order to look at some pigs.

'I think it's over a league from the town,' he had told me.

'Because of this constant pain in my stomach, it really is not worth the trouble for me to go and see pigs,' I said to myself, deciding to forgo this visit. Instead, I took the horse carriage for a spin around the neighbourhood in the company of the innkeeper. The latter made me the following suggestion:

'What about going to see the Liao He River?'[139] When we left the carriage and approached the riverbank, my eyes were dazzled by the scene. From its colour, one could have sworn it was an enormous waterway after a flood. Greyish elements from far off were swept along with the current and with tremendous force. When I went to Harbin, I asked Kito about this and he explained that since ancient times, the loan, or loess, of Manchuria had been carried by the winds and currents, year by year, ever further towards the sea. The geologists calculated that in fifty thousand years, the present Bay of Bohai[140] would be completely filled in. From the riverbank, I gazed at the stretch of water that separated the two sides and saw an agitated substance, more mud than water, unstoppably swept along on its way.

'In about fifty thousand years, the mouth of the river should be completely obstructed. However, a 3000-ton steamer can still move gently up the river without difficulty,' explained Kito.

It emerged from his remarks that the Chinese rivers were apathetic where human beings were concerned. Since time immemorial, the Chinese had drunk the muddy water, brought children into the world, and yet – up to the present at least – prospered.

A boat known as a *sampan*[141] was moving about in the waters. It had hoisted a sail that looked far too big in proportion to the size of the vessel. A number of thin bamboo rods had been fixed horizontally along the back of the sail. Perhaps it was just because of the ungainly shape of these corners, but whenever the sail was raised and unfurled, it made a considerable noise. It was a spectacle that could never be seen in Japan. We crossed the river and reached the opposite bank. There was nothing over there – only the railway station. It was a stopping place for the Beijing Express, so a lot of passengers boarded there. When I looked at the third-class carriages, I could not see a single seat. People were sleeping higgledy-piggledy on the floor of the train. We returned on a *sampan*, carried along by the muddy current as we crossed the river. I was told that in windy weather, the crossing was unpleasant. When spring arrived, mountainous blocks of ice were carried along the river. Since it was impossible to see any of what was taking place down stream, one paid with one's life if the vessel got jammed between two such blocks. At certain moments, when the route grew icebound, it was necessary to step out on to the ice, leaving the vessel to drift away on the waves, and then make one's way to the other side before boarding again. The innkeeper was recounting to me the stories of his own life.

The *sampan* drew up along the shore in a peculiar place. The bank was covered in reeds. There was no stone retaining wall: the dike consisted only of reeds. I was told that otherwise there was a risk that the current would sweep away the structure. The reeds seemed to absorb the water, as if there were no cause for concern at all, and as though no problems would arise, no matter what the quantity of water. Following a narrow path, we found ourselves right in the middle of a Chinese town. A curious smell assailed my nostrils. I suffered some minutes of chest pains. I had taken a sachet of powder out of my pocket, intending to swallow it. Unfortunately, there was no water at my disposal. Later on, common sense enabled me to discover how, in desperation, one could swallow powder even without the aid of any liquid. But, at that moment, I was not yet such an experienced patient in this respect, and I implored the innkeeper, with clasped hands, to find some water for me. He replied: 'All right, that's easy!'

He then treated me very roughly, dragging me about here, there, and everywhere. It was quite hard to bear, and I ended up curled into a ball on the roadside. Finally, we entered a shop. After having crossed an inner garden where *bonsai* were growing, I was taken into a corner room. But there was not the slightest drop of water.

'This way!' I was told, receiving an invitation to go up to the first floor of the building.

Climbing the stairs like caterpillars, we came to a corridor and entered a room. It contained two or three Japanese men engaged in a business discussion.

'Please do take a seat!' someone said to me, offering me a chair.

Later, after we had introduced ourselves, I discovered that the person who had welcomed me with the words 'Please take a seat!' and who had run to fetch me some water was named Kurata and was employed by the firm of Nisshin Mamekazu, soy cake specialists. Kurata confided to me that he had come from Japan half for pleasure, and half to conduct an inspection tour. For the latter purpose, he had travelled as far as Ying Kō.[142] I had never imagined that the need for a remedy would lead me to go begging for water at the end of the corridor on the first floor of a house where Nisshin Mamekazu had offices. In places like this, drinking water was not easy to find. The same was true of boiling water.

'I will go and prepare the tea,' said a young servant, energetically setting to work.

I was annoyed with the innkeeper; however, for the sake of appearances I had to converse with Kurata.

'Since soybeans are now sent to Dairen by rail, has the amount transported by river boat decreased?' I asked, striving to seem knowledgeable.

41

The subject of the conversation was as follows: did Hashimoto have a state-recognized doctorate or not? While we were staying at the Hotel Yamato in Dairen, he had received a sealed letter from the Railway Company. Looking with a strange expression at the meticulously written address on the envelope – 'Mr Hashimoto, Doctor of Agronomy' – the latter turned towards me and said with a sardonic laugh:

'You know, I don't like this at all!'

I wondered what could be the reason for this behaviour. Why did it embarrass him to be called 'doctor' when he made a show of being a scientist? I could not comprehend his attitude. If it really did suit him to be called 'doctor', then he should have become one! We let the matter rest.

It goes without saying that I thought Hashimoto was a doctor of agronomy. Zekō thought so, too. In fact, whenever I heard Zekō speaking of him to others, he clarified: 'Hashimoto? Yes, you mean the doctor of agronomy.'

As for me, I remembered having been definitely informed by the newspaper when Hashimoto had obtained his doctorate. Thus, from the moment we left Dairen and were heading North, I was fully conscious of being the travelling companion of a doctor honoured by the nation. Now, day after day, evening after evening, as we ate from the same pot and picked at the same food with our chopsticks, Hashimoto had started exclaiming whenever an opportunity arose:

'I do not have a doctorate, do you know that?'

At those moments, although Hashimoto might swear up and down that he had no Ph.D., I just said: 'Oh, really?'. In reality, I was astonished and quite unable to grasp the situation. I thought it could not be right for this man to have been teaching for ten years as a university professor without holding a doctorate, besides which I was sure I had read in the paper that a ceremony had been held when the doctorate was conferred. I contradicted him as much as I could manage. But I was dumbfounded by his persistence in saying he was not a 'doctor'. So, having no alternative, I accepted what he said and gave up. From then on, I started to grow sorry for him.

However, this world being what it is – full of unthinking beings wherever we go – people said 'Doctor Hashimoto, Doctor Hashimoto!' whenever it came into their heads. That is just what I noticed when I read the paper from time to time. They referred to 'Dr Hashimoto'. Finally, I got tired of remarking: 'Hey! They've called you a "doctor" again, you know!'

Hashimoto also feigned ignorance. Nevertheless, however innocent he chose to appear, it was impossible for him always to deceive people by saying 'I am not a "doctor"!' I had a similar experience. On the boat from Busan[143] to Shimonoseki, when I made the acquaintance of the wife of Hachirō of the Colonies Company,[144] the latter introduced me to Mrs Hachirō by saying with a perfectly serious face:

'This is Dr Natsume.'

His wife courteously replied with a deferential bow:

'Your name is already known to me.'

I then found myself obliged to greet her in the doctoral manner, saying:

'Ah, very good!' just like that.

It was therefore no surprise that Hashimoto should have become accustomed to being called 'Doctor' while travelling across Manchuria, on the way to Korea. Once Hashimoto had modified his position, I, too, began to feel a 'doctoral status' as the days progressed. Taking the Andong line,[145] we arrived safe and sound in that province. There, something occurred which annoyed me concerning Hashimoto's doctoral title. No doubt making a mistake, the receptionist attached to my bag a label reading: 'Hand baggage: property of Dr Hashimoto.' I was angry, but it would have been embarrassing to say anything, so I put up with it. At the next hotel, Hashimoto and I took separate rooms. And when Hashimoto's luggage was sent to the station, the young luggage porter at the hotel, convinced that my elegant leather bag belonged to my companion, carried it to the train double quick.

'It's no joke!' I protested.

Hashimoto, finding the situation comical, burst out laughing. 'That means people don't yet take you for a "doctor".' [146]

42

'Here we are,' said Hashimoto.

We alighted from the train. It was pitch dark. I had no idea where we were and could not get my bearings. The reference point was the station, which was so tiny that it resembled a single stall at a fairground. When I moved away from under the overhanging roof of the building, I experienced an even more intense feeling of sadness. The sky was starlit. Up high, the stars were the sole source of light, and our feet remained in darkness. We walked along the permanent way. The rails, lit by a lantern over a distance of about one-and-a-half metres, showed a dewy glimmer, followed by renewed darkness. Apart from this, there was nothing to be seen. We soon turned off to the right, and I got the impression that we were gradually descending a level.[147] After six or seven steps, I felt I was once more treading normally.

'We are back on level ground!' I remarked

At this junction I heard the singing of insects. It was not the warm rippling sound that one usually hears near one's house in Japan. When I realized that it was the hum of insects, I could hear it from every direction. We were walking by the light of a lantern carried by somebody in front; from all around us came sounds of the countless insects swarming in the plain.

When I think back on it now, the scene is fraught with charm and poetry. While writing this account of it, I see before my eyes the vast steppe described in Wei Shuzi's legend, *A Great Iron Mantle*.[148] Nevertheless, I found it hard to walk along that road. I felt as if I had consumed a portion of *tofu*,[149] cut up in cubes, that had turned into blocks of lime as soon as I swallowed them and obstructed my stomach. My throat was tight. I was salivating uncontrollably. In this condition, I was overcome by a feeling of nausea. That is, attempting to attain a calmer state in my mouth, I tried to fight against the desire to vomit. My legs grew tense, and I could no longer move them. A number of times, I thought about resting my painful posterior on the ground, amid the chirping insects. But I was reluctant to cause Hashimoto anxiety. Even if the porters were to receive the mistaken impression that I was doing my business in the grass, it would hardly have seemed a credible feat. So I forced myself to walk.

A long way off I saw a light. The road under my feet was flat. The light shone straight ahead. I assumed that was the spot where we were headed, and I walked along in silence beneath the stars. At midday, when we were in Ying Kō, I declined the invitation to have lunch with Sugihara of the Shōkin Bank. In the evening, I had refused to attend the banquet that had been organized by Amakasu. Then, like a fugitive, I told Hashimoto:

'Well, in view of my condition, I am revising my plans for an excursion to the Jian Shan Mountains.'

The fact was that my state of health was so disquieting that I had been forced to change my plans. I then realized that the spot of light that I saw ahead indicated the house for which we were destined that night and I proceeded straight across the desolate steppe. With the exception of the lamps, nothing tangible could be seen there, and a feeling of discouragement came over me. When I asked my guide whether it was an inn, he replied in the affirmative. As the programme drawn up by Hashimoto mentioned that Dang Gang Zu[150] was a thermal spa, I was quite prepared for the existence of the source of hot water underneath this brushwood-covered plain. However, I should never have expected such a desolate place to contain a peaceful-looking inn.

Finally, we reached the spot where the lamp was shining. It was a Western-style, single-storey building. The floor was level with the ground, so the house was quite low-built. Naturally, we wore our shoes when entering and leaving the floored rooms. The servants of the inn all wore straw sandals. It was a sober-looking house that gave the same impression up close as it had when viewed from a distance. I wondered whether it was inhabited or whether a light had been lit in an empty house, where carpentry work was yet to be completed. Entering the large room, we immediately noticed an organ that had been forgotten by its owner, a thing we never would have expected. Proceeding along the entire length of a dark corridor and then turning right, we were guided to a room situated in a wing of the building. The room was divided into two parts: the parquet-floored lower part contained upright chairs, a table, and a light-coloured easy chair.

The raised part of the room was covered with *tatami* mats that had been patched just as they would have been in Japan. This arrangement, in which one passed from one level to another, reminded me of Japanese houses where one steps up from a hard-packed floor to a *tatami*-carpeted room. I immediately stretched out full-length on the *tatami*. About half an hour later, the meal was brought. Hashimoto urged me to take some nourishment:

'Come on! Get up! Come and get supper!'

But it was in vain. I did not rise. Most of all, I could not look at any of the food that had been served. I did not even have the strength to open my eyes.

43

As soon as they awoke, Hashimoto and his friends loudly expressed their opinions as to whether or not the horses would arrive. There were three of them, so they needed three horses. In this vast steppe, catching three horses was doubtless no easy task. In vain, this band of three moaned more loudly than ever, complaining that they would never get started, despite not being particularly early risers themselves. Since I had given up the idea of accompanying them myself, I maintained an icy calm concerning their problems. In reality, it was quite clear that we had come here specifically intending to visit the Jian Shan mountain range. But once I had decided to stay behind, I felt annoyed that the others were going as planned. In the first place, Hashimoto himself was a specialist in agronomy, so for him it was certainly not necessary to go and see those mountains. The temple, built in the Dang era, was still intact, but there was nothing to be seen there except mountains, valleys, rocks, the temple, and the priests. There were neither cattle nor pigs. Therefore, it was not a place necessary for a professor of agronomy to tour on horseback. Of course, it did not occur to me to tell him my views on the matter or to use them as a pretext for getting him to change his plans. I therefore let him act as he intended. To my astonishment, three horses arrived in accordance with their request. I did not even try to enquire where they had come from. What was certain was that there they were. The three companions valiantly rushed out, as though spurred on by exasperation. I became the sole occupant of the two rooms in Western and Japanese style, and, since there was nothing else to do, I prepared for a whole day of quiet rest. First and foremost,

I thought that lying down would be just as restorative as taking medication, and so I stretched out full-length on a fur, not knowing whether it was fox or badger. As soon as I had done so, I heard Hashimoto's voice through the window: 'Hey! Could you come out here for a minute?'

Telling myself that there was bound to be something wrong, I went out on to the plain as requested, just as I was, in straw sandals, without pausing to put on any shoes. In the midst of a place resembling a vast prairie, there were three horses. Since each was of the small packsaddle type, it was a very welcome sight. One of them was clearly refusing to be mounted by Ōshige. Whenever he approached the horse, it kicked and reared its head.

'It's because the animal's frightened!' said a young Chinese servant, who had made blinders with a towel.

Using both hands, he held the horse firmly by the bit. Observed from a distance, it seemed as if the horse was wearing a headband, and it was a funny sight. When Ōshige approached the horse, smiling grimly, it was still funnier. We watched this sequence of events recur again and again. The horse was extremely reluctant to oblige its rider, so the matter was by no means easily settled. Each of us tried to outdo the others in applause. Since Hashimoto came from the Hokkaidō region, he mounted without difficulty, and the other person knew how to hold a horse by the reins. (I have forgotten his name, so I am calling him 'the other person'. I only remember that he was the one responsible for the Xiong Yue Zheng tree nursery and that he had once been Hashimoto's pupil.)

At that moment, standing in the field, I wondered whether my reason for declining to take part in the tour to the Jian Shan Mountains might not actually be a desire to keep intact my reputation as a horseman.

However, without allowing my facial expression to betray my feelings in any way, I watched regretfully as the three men departed. Judging from Ōshige's posture on his horse, I presumed that the prospect of the ride all the way to the Jian Shan Mountains was causing him some anxiety, and I was seized with pity. Hashimoto spurred his horse on, having declared that he would be back that same evening. The man in charge of the tree nursery followed him, not allowing himself to be outdone. Ōshige was the only one who lagged behind. The horse was still wearing blinkers. Very soon, two silhouettes disappeared into the sorghum. I no longer knew what direction they had taken. Ahead of me, the tall Chinese who were moving about in the vicinity likewise became concealed by the sorghum. They carried long rifles suspended from their shoulders. When I first saw them, they reminded me of the mounted Manchurian bandits. They disappeared into the sorghum like Hashimoto and, in fact, at almost the same time. A few moments later, I heard an explosion. Immediately afterwards, while images passed before me of the serious accident that would occur if the tall silhouettes came anywhere near the three men, I returned to my room and fell asleep on the badger skin.

<u>44</u>

Armed with a towel, I made my way to the hot spring. I had to cover about a hundred metres across the plain. To reach the interior of the establishment, with its stone floors, I first went down three wooden planks. Finally, I reached the hot spring. The baths had been constructed by the army during the military regime,[151] and instead of using an aesthetically pleasing design, they had been assembled with a total lack of taste. The regulations, still displayed at the entrance, stated that it was forbidden to remain in the bath for more than a quarter of an hour. I tried an array of different positions in the baths, knowing full well that I was breaking the regulations: I sat on the stone stairs; I padded around on all fours; I leaned against the wall and held my head in my arms; and finally I went outside, walked around the building, and noticed a large pond in the back. There, a young man who had boarded a shabby vessel approached me, energetically waving a boat hook.

'Say! Does this pond have hot spring water or just ordinary water?' I asked him.

The young man, assuming a remarkably sullen expression, replied: 'It's hot water!'

Since the fellow was being so unpleasant, I no longer addressed him. From the edge of the pond, I looked down through the water to the bottom. From time to time, something resembling moss floated up to the surface. I wondered whether it was just vapour. I felt inclined to ask, to set my mind at rest, whether there were any fish in this pond. But my interlocutor, such as he was, had turned on his heel and walked away. I then returned to the inn. A little while later, learning that the pond did indeed contain fish swimming about in it, I was amazed. What astonished me even further was learning that not a single drop of water came out of this pond.

There was yet another surprise in store for me. On returning from the spa, when I entered the main hall, intending to return to my room, I noticed a woman whom I had never met before. I did not know where she had come from. From her full, purple trousers, to the sound made by her boots and her manner of walking about the house, one could have sworn she was a teacher, or else a student. In Tokyo, since it was the capital, one would only have to go out on to the street to see such women. But in this vast plain, no spot could have been found where such an ornament — where a person with such lustre would appear. For a length of time, I gazed at this woman's silhouette with an awkward expression on my face.

Back in my room, I once again fell asleep. On waking, I heard the hum of insects outside the window. As melancholy overcame me, I went into the Western-style room, sat in the armchair, and began to sing Nō theatre pieces. Naturally, my performance was completely unrehearsed. The chambermaid came to see me. I asked her about the woman I had just seen.

'It's probably someone I know,' she said straight out.

After supper, I had begun smoking a cigarette, when suddenly I heard the sound of the organ in the drawing-room. I asked whether it might by chance be the woman in question.

'No, no! It's the evening chambermaid,' I was told.

Never would I have expected to find such highly cultivated chambermaids in this steppe. I was told that the woman with the full trousers had departed.

I remained alone, sitting in the armchair, oblivious of everything until the approach of dusk, when the plain changed to a colour that gave the impression of coldness. All of a sudden, amidst the quiet of the steppe, I heard a charming voice say:

'Please! Come and relax a little: I'm all alone, you know!'

Judging from the inflections of the voice, it was most certainly a native of Tokyo. I quickly rose and looked outside. Unfortunately, the window was covered with muslin netting. I opened it quickly and put my head out. Twilight covered the whole of the steppe, and the woman's silhouette was obscured by the bluish haze. I did not know who she was.

Hashimoto's little party returned in the evening. Informed by the chambermaid, I went out the back door and saw a bean-shaped distant light. The chambermaid announced: 'There they are!'

The space being so vast, I had to ask whether the light we saw was Hashimoto's or someone else's.

'No, no! It is them!' she assured me.

It was true indeed. The light came from a lantern carried by the Chinese. He had left the inn in the evening in order to go and meet the three friends. Hashimoto left his horse at the door of the inn and confided to me:

'Oh! It was such an ordeal! And the place wasn't even worth it!' He said Ōshige had fallen off his horse three times.

45

'When you get to Mukden,[152] it would be a good thing to call in at the offices of the Railway Company!' Zekō had told us before our departure [see Plate 16].

As the famous *haiku* writer Rokkotsu[153] apparently lived there, I had the cunning thought that it would not be a bad idea at all to pay him some attention as well. However, I was travelling in the company of Hashimoto. After discussing the matter, therefore, we both decided that it would show good breeding to make a little fuss over Rokkotsu. A carriage was sent from the inn to fetch us from the station. Its colour was very unusual: it looked as though it had been dug out of the mud and dried in the bright sunlight. As soon as he had left the grounds of the station, his carriage loaded with passengers and luggage, the coachman violently cracked his whip, making a most unpleasant sound. He behaved more roughly than a stagecoach driver going up a hill. The road was not very wide, particularly as we approached the fortified enclosure: the road that until now had spread freely in the vast plain began to narrow, with shops lining each side. Not only was the railway carriage moving at top speed, but the formidable whip swished continuously over our heads. The coachman spurred the horse on with excessive vehemence.

We were in Mukden, so there were many people passing both to the right and to the left of the carriage [see Plate 18]. I saw six mules hitched to a wagon. From their slow pace, they could have been oxen. It was quite dangerous! Despite this, the coachman was still driving at full speed, as if we were travelling across some deserted region. For people like us, who love tranquillity, it was veritable torment to be transported in such a carriage. The coachman, of course, let his oily, dust-laden Chinese pigtail flap in the air, now and then muttering some remark in the Manchu tongue. Frowning, I looked at everything in the street that was not blocked by the horse. His attempts to please his passengers by needlessly whipping the raw-boned horse reminded me of the master of a house who reprimands his wife in order to treat his guests as well as possible.

Returning from Beiling[154] and approaching the hotel, I saw a dark mass on the left, formed by a crowd of people. In this quarter of town, dirty Chinese shops full of vegetables, cheese, meat pies, and Chinese *tofu* were packed together tightly in rows. Looking to see what was hidden beneath the mass of dark heads, I discovered a man, perhaps sixty years old, seated on the ground. His folded legs were what had drawn the crowd's attention. Over a stretch of slightly more than five centimetres, somewhere between the left knee and the foot, the flesh hung down from the bone and was shrivelled up as though it had been violently torn off. It looked as if a pomegranate had been thrown at him and its seeds crushed. Our guide, although he must have been accustomed to this kind of spectacle, seemed mildly frightened: he immediately stopped the carriage and asked a question in Chinese. Although I did not understand a word, I listened intently and twice asked: 'What's happening? What's happening?'

Astonishing though it may seem, the Chinese who had crowded round in a dense mass all looked at the wound without uttering a word. They were all perfectly calm and made not the slightest movement. What struck me still more forcibly was the fact that no particular emotion was visible on the face of the old man, who supported himself by leaning with his hands on the ground behind him, displaying his wound to all around. He showed no sign of pain; neither did he show any sadness. This did not mean that he appeared apathetic. I noticed his eyes. There seemed to be a veil covering the eyes of this old man seated on the ground.

'They say he was hit by a vehicle,' the guide explained.

'Isn't there a doctor anywhere? Wouldn't it be a good idea to fetch one?' I said, urging my interlocutor to take action.

'Yes, yes! Something ought to be done soon!' my guide replied.

The latter had now resumed his usual air. Without hesitating, the dust-covered coachman then once again cracked his whip, driving the horses on like a maniac, unconcerned with people, other vehicles, and the road. When I reached the entrance to the hotel, my hat and my suit were coated with yellow dust, and I felt relieved at having at last broken off all connection with those cruel Chinese.

46

The exterior of this old Chinese house had never been altered. From the outside, it looked like the chief sanctuary of a Buddhist temple. Inside, partition walls had been added to create separate reception areas for guests. Proceeding along the outer corridor attached to the building, I cast a furtive glance at the drawing-room opposite me and noticed lots of bric-a-brac. I wondered what it could be. Later, I learned that a second-hand goods dealer, who had travelled to Beijing on a hunt for bargains, had stayed here on the way back and set up shop. I had a look around just for fun and then, when it started getting late, went out into the street again.

This time, a rickshaw had been placed at our disposal and I began to feel calmer, telling myself that everything would pass satisfactorily. Imitating 'high society people', or the 'High Collars',[155] I crossed my legs and threw out my chest. In reality, it was no joke! The rickshaw is a Japanese invention; however, when it is drawn by Chinese or Koreans, one can no longer rest. They regard the rickshaw as a foreign invention and have a way of jerking it about that shows a lack of respect for this mode of transportation. When I went to Hai Zheng[156] to view the relics of the ancient state of Koma, my posterior was so badly tossed about on the seat of a rickshaw that I felt very uncomfortable. At least once every hundred metres, it seemed I was thrown thirty metres up into the air. I was treated so badly that I wanted to box the Korean's ears. But since the Mukden streets were not as badly dented as those of Hai Zheng, the acrobatics I was forced to perform did not torment me quite as badly. However, the rickshaw driver certainly showed no skill in the way in which he pulled his vehicle. His idea that his task was to gallop along without exercising any judgement was also very characteristic of the Koreans. While being bumped about, I thought to myself that any rickshaw driver who does not give proper consideration to his passengers' nerves cannot be called a competent professional, even if he is a good runner.

Meanwhile, we passed through a magnificent gate in the shape of a tower. I remembered having passed through it a number of times during the four days I spent in Mukden. I heard its name frequently, but have since completely forgotten it. Its shape is also very hazy in my mind; however, when I first entered Mukden and lifted my eyes towards the top of the tower and the dust-covered roofs, I let loose an exclamation. The impressions of that day are still firmly imprinted on my mind. When Hashimoto and I went to buy calligraphic brushes and ink in a little shop near the gateway, I had another memorable experience. Hashimoto stepped over the threshold and entered the shop. I got ready to follow him. Proceeding until I was half-way under the awning, I prepared to enter, when suddenly I noticed one of the characteristic smells of Manchuria. I retreated by two steps and re-entered the street. The gate that I mentioned was about twenty metres from the crossroads where I was standing. I raised my hand and looked at it intently.

The day was drawing to a close, so the sun no longer lit up the roof tiles; neither did any shiny part of the edifice stand out. The whole of it hovered solemnly over the town and its noisy intersections. There was nothing original in the architecture of the tower, except for the old part. The roofs and the tiles had all blended into more or less the same colour. Only the little roof bells[157] were coloured greyish-green, as if by a skilful hand. I could see tall grass sprouting up between the broken tiles. The shadow thrown by the peak of my cap fell across two white pigeons. For the first time in ages, I felt a sudden urge to compose a real Chinese poem.[158] While waiting for Hashimoto, I started trying to write something. But, before I had succeeded in producing a single line, Hashimoto reappeared from the shop, tightly clutching ink and brushes at his side. All pleasure in poetical composition immediately vanished.

Apart from that, the only thing that this tour brought me was a depressing feeling caused by all the dust that had fallen on me from the bricks above and by the fear that I would never be able to re-emerge from this damp, vault-like place. Passing through this dingy gateway, the rickshaw man conveyed me as far as the offices of the Railway Company, which were located inside the fortified enclosure. His villainy was unequalled. I rose and fell in the rickshaw as if I had been a living package wrapped in a carrying sack.[159]

47

When I drank the tea, it tasted salty and pungent. Finding this a little strange, I put the bowl down and listened to Hashimoto completely at my leisure. He explained that Mukden had been without drains since ancient times. Needless to say, when it comes to two natural functions, urination and defecation, this was a considerable disadvantage. Inevitably, the ground had for countless centuries been saturated with urine and excrement, and Hashimoto said that the disastrous results were still noticeable in the drinking water. Generally speaking, he was right. In scientific terms, however, his explanations struck me as slightly faulty. In the first place, assuming such a problem had arisen, how could the crops grow? With my birdbrain, however, I was incapable of producing any solid arguments in support of my thesis. Even Hashimoto warned me that the origins of this story were somewhat legendary; apparently, it was something similar to the story of the Barbarians of the East and Yamato Dake no Mikoto.[160] Apart from the problem of factual accuracy, there is no doubt that it had actually become a part of history and that people had given it a good deal of importance. The Chinese are a very dirty people.

When I saw the bath that I had requested, I noticed that the water was cloudy. The deposits in the water were not particularly yellow, but judging from the taste of the tea, one could only suppose that it had been prepared with acidic boiling water. And although I had been supplied in Dairen with soybean soap that could dissolve in salt water, I preferred not to take them out of my luggage. The bathroom, like the bath itself, was small. The chambermaid then came in and started scrubbing my back. Though embarrassed at the idea of turning my body towards her, I started to converse:

'Are you Japanese? What region do you come from?' I asked her, among other questions.

In the beginning, when I arrived at the hotel, she had mistaken me for someone who had formed part of Hashimoto's escort.

'Well, well! You have come with Mr So-and-So!' she had said.

She told me that Mr So-and-So had spent the night here with Hashimoto when the latter had travelled to Mongolia. I did not try to find out from her whether she had made the mistake because our faces were similar or because I looked like a servant. Outside there was an enormous pot buried in the ground. Our sweat and dirt, mixed in with the acidic water, were poured into it morning and evening; the water sometimes accumulated there to such a level that if it was not drained off, it overflowed. A Chinese servant girl then took this water away somewhere in old petroleum jelly cans, suspended from a palanquin. While taking my bath, I wondered exactly where they took this water. Perhaps my anxiety was excessive, but I felt quite disconcerted when I imagined the measures they might be taking to get rid of this wastewater. [161]

In addition, they also brought in a meal that was far too large. Anybody with stomach trouble like me only had to look at what was served on the table to feel immediately that he had already had enough. The bedding we were given for the night was damasked. At the reception desk, the telephone rang incessantly. The distinguished-looking proprietress kept answering:

'Yes? Hullo, hullo!'

On one occasion, I had a craving for chocolate cake. When I asked the chambermaid whether there was any to be had, the proprietress immediately telephoned – calling 'Hullo, hullo,' and arranged for some to be sent. Whenever we went to have lunch in the offices of the Railway Company, champagne appeared.

When we paid a courtesy visit to the British Consulate, we saw that a photograph of the King of England was hung respectfully on the wall. I sensed a real London atmosphere. In contrast, opposite the corridor leading to the Japanese-style drawing rooms, there was a blank white wall. A ray of light slanted down it from the high window. There was nothing to be done. However, the transparent sheet of paper fixed to the window bore something in Chinese, as if it came from the *Tale of the Three Kingdoms*, as shown on the prints of Hokusai.[162] It was not very pleasing to look at. In addition, the room gave off a strange odour. It was a clinging smell that the Chinese leave behind them on their departure and that persists, however hard the fanatically clean Japanese try to remove it. I was told that this inn, near the station, was soon to be transferred to a new location. This odour would then probably disappear. It had to be accepted, however, that the acidic tea was inseparable from the curse that had fallen upon the men and cattle of Mukden.

48

Two black pillars towered above us. The panels of the door were also painted black. The rivets were as big as overturned tea or rice bowls. I never would have imagined that such a door, looking as if it belonged to the magnificent dwelling of a prince, could be found standing in the middle of a Chinese town. After opening it, we came to another, constructed in the Chinese style. After passing through the second one and proceeding through a cemented thoroughfare some two metres wide, we arrived at the front of the house,[163] flanked by buildings on either side. The garden, resembling a square box, was quite empty. Walking along this roofless middle road, we came to a house at the very end. I learned, listening to the explanation given by Rokkotsu, that at the end of the passage there was a traditional dwelling, a '*Zheng fang*', facing south, as well as side buildings, '*Xiang fang*', on either hand, facing east and west. According to Rokkotsu, certain rooms had been arranged entirely in Japanese style.

'Come with me for a moment and have a look,' Rokkotsu said.

He showed me the way and I followed him. We then arrived quite unexpectedly at the main entrance. At the back of the next room, which was covered with *tatami* mats, I caught sight of a magnificent *kakemono*.[164] 'Well, well!' I said to myself. My guide opened the side door of the building on the left.

'Here,' he said, 'you see there is a big reception hall in the Chinese style.'

To my astonishment, it was furnished with sandalwood chairs. They differed from the usual Western style in that they did not encumber the middle of the room. They were arranged throughout the room in an orderly fashion. Guests would not find it possible, on their arrival, to sit down facing one another, so I assumed that they would sit side by side in this manner. The room also contained two seats that must have been laboriously installed: they resembled thrones for kings. A square, red cushion had been placed on each of them.

'The Chinese are really quite happy-go-lucky people,' Rokkotsu explained. 'They just lean like this to discuss things and do business.'

He was well-versed in Chinese customs and thoroughly grasped everything concerning that country.

At one moment, he decided to defend the Chinese pigtail custom. His arguments were that when the Chinese wore their traditional clothes of soft texture, it gave them an extremely pleasant feeling to leave a long mane of hair draping down over brightly coloured material. For this reason, things should be left alone. Actually, I was quite surprised at Rokkotsu's use of the expression: 'give an extremely pleasant feeling'. My surprise lasts to this day when I think back on his words. It may be because on one occasion, when I saw hanging down from the neck of a grimy old man something that resembled a sparse moustache shaped like a slug, it cast considerable doubt on the appropriateness of the phrase 'extremely pleasant feeling'.

It was in a similar spirit that Rokkotsu also tolerated the Western style of the big reception rooms of the traditional Chinese residence. In the adjacent dining-room, we were served a European meal. After this, we played billiards in our shirt sleeves. There was certainly nothing very Chinese about such a scene. By comparison with everything I had heard from Hashimoto concerning Rokkotsu, the latter in reality seemed to have twice as much drive and spirit. The expression 'gave an extremely pleasant feeling' was perhaps a little exaggerated. Rokkotsu had lost a leg in the war, the left one – or perhaps it was the right. Now he could get up and sit down without any awkwardness, to such an extent that one would never even notice it. Also, he affected the working-class speech of Tokyo, which was inappropriate for a military man. When I asked him where he was born, he said his birthplace was Kanda. Kanda?[165] Yes, it was quite possible. In a word, Rokkotsu, while loving China, was far removed from it and its nature.

'There is a spare room, do stay!' he said insistently.

Replying 'Yes, we may have difficulty with our arrangements for the return journey!' and complying on the spot would probably have been a good idea.

'According to our programme, we are to return to Mukden by the train that departs in the middle of the night,' put in Hashimoto.

Rokkotsu then immediately repeated his offer of lodging. 'Yes, well – if there is such a train, I am sorry!' he said.

Then he reverted to his suggestion by saying:

'If you take another train, it would be all right, wouldn't it?'

Since unfortunately I did not slavishly adhere to the programme, I had no alternative but to acquiesce, subject to conditions: 'If there is no night train, I shall ask you for your hospitality for one night.'

Rokkotsu then once again agreed.

Now, since we did take the night train as planned, I did not in the end have occasion to spend the night in the company office building. The bedrooms are the only part of it that I am unacquainted with.

49

When we turned to the right and reached a vast place that could hardly have been taken for a road, I finally felt reassured. I thought that here there was no longer any reason to fear being crushed to death. On the way, I conversed with the lead messenger boy from the hotel, who acted as my guide. There is no doubt that the Manchurian sun causes the animals' coats to shine in the autumn,[166] as people say. No matter how firmly I pulled my cap onto my head, the visor, shaped like a half-moon, gave me no protection against the sun from my cheeks down to the ground. There was nothing to be done. The sun shone straight down and burned painfully. The light dust stirred up by the horse's hooves flew about in the hidden places under the carriage. The hotel messenger said joyfully:

'It's magnificent weather! If the wind were blowing, it would not be nearly so pleasant.'

Very soon, the carriage left the houses behind and drove out into the vast plain. As it was the steppe, there naturally was no vegetation to be seen. But when one looked into the distance, a kind of bluish tint in harmony with the season seemed to burst forth from every spot as far as the eye could see, forming a multicoloured shadow. Why was this stretch of land so empty? For a native of Tokyo, for whom the view at home is blocked by countless houses, this question is bound to spring to mind. But this time, after having travelled through places peopled by stiff and starchy inhabitants, I found myself overcome by an impression of freshness instead of by this question. Needless to say, there was no route, in the usual sense of the word. It was a road created by nature, stretching towards all four points of the compass simultaneously; the tracks of the carriages took directions according to their own imagination and to the fancy of travellers.

A carriage driven by Chinese made its appearance. Inside this vehicle, which resembled a coffin and had a semi-cylindrical roof, there sat a woman whose hair was set with oil. The shafts of the carriage were short, but its wheels were thick and solidly constructed. Needless to say, the carriage was drawn by a mule. It inevitably reminded me of the ox wagons so popular in Japan in former times. But the vehicle that caught my eye was far more luxurious than an ox wagon; however, it seemed to me that this vehicle's passenger was having a very uncomfortable ride. Watching the way in which it moved, I was tempted to use the term 'jostling along'. I am not very familiar with the exact meaning of the Chinese characters denoting this expression;[167] however, I thought the passenger in this vehicle was most certainly being 'jostled'. There was no doubt about it. To tell the truth, though, it is not only Chinese carriages that bounce along. My own conveyance was equally problematic. You could have said in indifferent tones: 'The plain extends as far as the eye can see, doesn't it?' And it certainly did look flat. But if I had been told, 'It will take a while, but we shall try and get through,' then I would have perceived all the terrible bumps from afar.

'I say! Isn't the carriage likely to turn over here?' I asked the hotel employee in anxious tones.

He replied without exhibiting the slightest sense of danger: 'No! It will be all right, I expect.'

The employee's seat, which seemed to be at the same level as my own, suddenly rose. I thought he was going to slip off it and fall on to me. Then the reverse happened. I very nearly fell over on to the man's hat. It was most unpleasant. My nerves were in a fragile state, so I wanted to get off whenever the carriage tossed. Despite this, the coachman, in accordance with his regular habit, and taking no notice of his passengers' mood, continued at a gallop, without any fear of rivals keeping up with him. When I had become more and more anxious and had started thinking to myself, 'This is really pointless!', we reached a place where the state of the road suddenly worsened. For no reason apparent to me, there were thirty or forty distinct carriage tracks to be seen on the ground. Also, the width of the ruts was about fifteen to twenty centimetres. If one looked carefully, one could see that they were quite deep. The ruts blocked the sunlight, so the bottoms were dark and black. Our coachman carefully drove through them. If everything had taken a normal course, it would have been all right. But on one side, the wheels penetrated the mud as if it had been butter, while on the other side of the carriage, they were running over ground as hard as before. My seat was on the side above the muddy part of the ground. All of a sudden the vehicle sank so far into the mud that my feet touched the ground. It seemed to me that the hotel clerk had been thrown over my head. Unable to stand it any longer, I jumped down into the mud.

50

The steppe rapidly gave place to a stretch of land covered with dense grass, causing me some astonishment. When I observed that if only trees had been growing there, the vegetation of this plain would be even denser, I noticed that the view from each side of the carriage was already blocked. They were not bamboo, but the height of the green masses made it look exactly like a bamboo grove. I had a sense of tranquillity, as if I had been walking in the Japanese countryside. Here and there, slender branches, rebelliously projecting from the main growth, intruded on to the roadway. It gave incomparable pleasure to walk along, bending one's head beneath the greenery. The road itself had become more regular than the one we had been travelling along a few moments earlier; we could clearly see its whiteness stretching behind the grass and the trees. In one place, tall pines rose up. Their needles were twice as long as those in Japan, and they were even darker than the pines that grow by the sea. In another place, I saw the traces of a pleasure garden. Arriving there, the eye could immediately take in, from the top of the carriage, a thicket covering a distance of about two hundred metres. An oblong tombstone stood opposite. Only its contours could be detected. Needless to say, I was unable to read the characters engraved on it.

A few moments later, the road came to an end and we reached a high doorway consisting of three arches constructed of stone slabs. To pass through it, we had to ascend a very high stone stairway. A dragon was sculpted in the wall on each side of the door.

'That is the main doorway, you see! But since it is closed, we have to go around,' the guide said.

The horse went up on to a kind of embankment. A brick wall appeared on the right. Certain parts of it were in ruins. On the left, in a little valley that sloped gently downwards, virgin vines and trees forming a copse succeeded one another in closely packed rows. The road was so narrow that it was only with difficulty that the carriage could proceed on its way. We went all the way around, then left the carriage and entered through a side door. My eyes were then completely soothed. Short grass sprouted forth here and there between the square flagstones that covered the ground in close succession, leading to a distant place where there were only pine trees.

At each step we took, our shoes reverberated as they came in contact with the stony ground. We had covered about a hundred metres when, turning towards the front of the building, we noticed a large stone elephant on each side of the door. The figures were quite large and imposing! Since they were stone, they presented a calming spectacle. At the end of our path, entering a place that resembled a tower, I found a large monument, erected in someone's memory, which had been placed on the back of a tortoise. The latter was likewise very large. The monument, however, was of impressive dimensions. The inscriptions were engraved in the stone in three languages: Mongol, Manchu, and Mandarin Chinese. When we arrived from the rear, I saw the Lung En Men door towering skywards. When I looked past the frame formed by the centre arches, I discovered a three-storied pagoda. The enclosure wall on both sides of the scene was also extraordinary.

'Hmm, I would enjoy a walk along that wall!' I said to the hotel employee.

'Yes, we shall be going up there! You'll see!' he replied, entering the building.

The interior was divided up into perfectly square rooms. Facing me was a temple consecrated to ancestor worship, and after ascending a stone stairway at the side, I came out on to the wall. The rear part of the temple was shaped like a half-moon. The wall continued all around the imperial tomb.

A young, bare-footed Chinese monk came towards us. He caught up with the hotel clerk and energetically whispered something in his ear. I asked the clerk what was happening.

'Nothing important!' he replied vaguely.

And then, after I had repeated my inquiry, he reluctantly told me. A ball of gold attached to the edge of a roof had fallen off and been picked up from the ground. This man had offered to sell it. It would not have been tolerable for this transaction to be conducted in public, so he had suggested that it should occur surreptitiously in the course of a sightseeing tour. The Chinese really are a cunning people, are they not?

The Chinese guardian of the imperial tomb was probably a cunning character as well, but the hotel clerk who spoke to me of buying this gold ball at a bargain price was not particularly honest either. He furtively got out the money and put the gold ball in his pocket.

While walking along the top of the wall, I saw a big tree down below.

'The mulberry trees grow as big as that!' said the hotel clerk, pointing at the tree.

It is true that one could not have reached around it even with both arms.

'How long is the wall on this side?' I asked my guide.

'Well, let us measure it!' he replied.

Counting one step as sixty centimetres, we took four steps. Glancing downwards, I saw the fruit of the red tree that climbed the wall. I have completely forgotten the length that the clerk calculated for the wall.

51

Fushun [see Plate 21] is a place where coal is mined. Hashimoto told me that the manager of the mine was a Mr Matsuda. He explained that he had got to know him on the boat when he had come to Manchuria. In response to the invitation he had given Hashimoto upon their introduction, Hashimoto had sent him a telegram telling him that he would be arriving the next day. On the train we saw two Westerners. Since it was morning, we ate the refreshments that we had brought with us. On reaching Fushun, we all alighted from the train. We went to meet the Westerners and performed our introductions. I then learned that one of them was the British Consul in Mukden. We all went to the offices of the mining company and met Mr Matsuda on the first floor. He wore a light-coloured suit over a crepe shirt. He had a direct manner and would never have been taken for the manager of the mine. He showed Hashimoto and me and then the two Englishmen to two different places and devoted the same amount of time to both parties. Neither Hashimoto nor I spoke in English. We therefore did not exchange a single word with the British people.

Very soon, Matsuda escorted us out of the room. When we went up on to the embankment where the water tower had been erected, I was able to take in the whole town at a glance. It had not yet been completed. But apart from the fact that all the buildings were brick, one would never have imagined from the architecture – which incidentally was worthy of illustration in the English journal *Studio*[168] – that this place was managed by Japanese. I was also astonished at how all or almost all of the neat little houses varied from one another in their appearance. For every ten houses, there were ten different colours. The buildings included a church, a theatre, a hospital, a school, and, needless to say, the miners' living quarters. They were all buildings that one would enjoy seeing on a walk through the suburbs of Tokyo. In reply to the question that we asked him, Matsuda informed us that they had been built exclusively by Japanese engineers.

When one looked away from the town and contemplated the low undulating hills visible in the opposite direction, one could see the tops of chimneys in two distant places. As these chimneys were separated by more than a league, it was clear that the mine extended over a considerable area. According to Matsuda's explanation, one found coal everywhere, no matter where one prospected, and it would be a century or two before the mine was exhausted. When we had lunch, I felt sorry for the English people who did not use chopsticks or eat rice. It was surprising that the British Consul, who had lived in China for eighteen years, was completely incapable of using chopsticks. On the other hand, he expressed himself remarkably well in Mandarin Chinese. Matsuda, who was very busy, left the table and was unable to return. The man who replaced him as our host had a difficult task, speaking to the British people in English and to us in Japanese. However, neither Hashimoto nor I myself made use of our English. The English, by nature, are stamped with arrogance, and, unless they have been introduced, are not very willing to talk to somebody from elsewhere. That is why we showed the same arrogance towards them.[169]

After the meal, we went on a tour of the interior of the mine. An engineer called Tajima acted as our guide. At the entrance, five safety lamps were lit[170] and five sticks were prepared; this equipment was divided between us. The gallery, each side of which measured about one metre and eight centimetres, sloped gently downwards. After about thirty metres, the darkness was impenetrable. As miners' lanterns only light up one's feet, the lighting was inadequate. However, contrary to what I had expected, the floor was flat. The ceiling, too, was fairly high. We turned to the right and groped our way along. All of a sudden, Tajima, who was just in front of me, came to a dead stop. I did likewise. Our guide had stopped, so everybody behind him did the same.

'There is a bench here. People visiting the mine generally rest for five or six minutes so that their eyes will become accustomed to the darkness,' Tajima informed us.

During this interval, we all examined each other's faces in the light of the lanterns. We were standing. Nobody sat down. Quiet reigned inside the mine, which, as the time passed, seemed very gloomy. Then Tajima said: 'That's better now, isn't it?'

And he immediately turned right again and went deeper and deeper into the mine. I did the same. So did the three others behind me.[171]

NOTES

1 The South Manchurian Railway Company (*Nan Manshu Tetsudo Kabushiki Kaisha*) was far more than a transportation company. As described in the Introduction, it played a fundamental role in the development of the Japanese presence in the Liaoning region, and in political, economic and cultural activities in Manchuria as a whole. All of these aspects of the SMR will become very clear in the pages of this travelogue. See the Introduction for further information on the history and activities of the SMR. Zekō Nakamura, a schoolfriend of Sōseki's, served as the second President of the SMR from 1908–14.

2 Kanda, the 'Latin Quarter' of Tokyo, is a district in Northeast Tokyo, particularly famous for its publishing houses and bookstores.

3 This is *tempura*, a dish consisting of deep-fried slices of vegetables, fish, or seafood served with rice. The dish is said to have originated in Portugal. In this passage, Sōseki contrasts this relatively inexpensive dish with the fancier fare of the Ogawa Restaurant.

4 In the original text, Sōseki uses the term '*Bakhan*', the ancient name given to Shimonoseki. This harbour town, in the Southwest corner of the main island of Honshū, faces Korea across the so-called Shimonoseki Strait.

5 The former name of Dalian (Daihi in Russian). Situated at the southeast corner of the Liaodong peninsula, it forms part of Lushun (Port Arthur). At the beginning of the twentieth century, Czarist Russia controlled this very important port; after the Russo-Japanese War, it came under the control of Japan. It now has more than 500,000 inhabitants.

6 Teiji Suzuki, an architect, was the husband of Sōseki's younger sister.

7 In Japan, all boat names end in -*maru*. Literally 'the town of Deiling'. Deiling is a town situated in Manchuria, north of Mukden (Shenyang), on the Trans-Manchurian railway.

8 Andong (Antong or Antō in Japanese) is a port town in Manchuria, situated on the right bank of the mouth of the Yalu river, close to the Korean frontier (now North Korea). The population of this town is now 420,000.

9 '*Ni hyaku tōka*', literally 'the two hundred and tenth day' after the beginning of spring, according to the lunar calendar. It is a fateful date, when peasants particularly fear the wind and rain because the early rice is in full flower. It is also called 'the day of storms'.

10 The Hotel Yamato stood on the edge of the largest public square in Dairen (see Plate 14). This building, purely Western in architectural style, belonged to the SMR. The name 'Yamato' historically signified one of the five ancient provinces of 'Kinai', those provinces nearest to the old capital that formed the imperial domains (now forming the department of Nara). The name 'Yamato' carried strong connotations of the original and traditional Japan, referring as it does to the historical heart and cradle of Japanese civilization in Asuka, Nara, and Kyoto. 'Yamato' also symbolizes the expansionist policy followed by Japan in Asia until 1945. The biggest Japanese warship, for example, the pride of the Imperial fleet, also bore the highly resonant name 'Yamato'.

11 A traditional square of Japanese fabric, often ornamented with various patterns. It was (and still is) used for wrapping and carrying objects by tying the four corners of the cloth together into a knot.

12 By 1909, the time when this travel report was written, Sōseki was already a famous writer. He had been a public figure since 1905, when *I am a Cat* achieved widespread popularity. See the Introduction for further information.

13 Kuroyanagi Kaishu was Sōseki's colleague at Upper High School No. 1 in Tokyo, the location of Sōseki's first teaching position.

14 Japanese has two writing systems to represent native words and sounds: the Chinese characters, or '*kanji*', borrowed from the sixth century onwards, and the syllabaries, or '*kana*', that made their appearance in the tenth century in Heian high society. *Kana* are simple phonetic signs: '*hiragana*' for the transcription of words of Japanese origin, and '*katakana*' for the transcription of terms of foreign origin. To these must be added the Roman alphabet, called '*rōmaji*', more and more commonplace in quotations, international transcriptions, and advertisements. The complexity of the Chinese characters stems largely from the fact that they sometimes have a number of interpretations and even pronunciations – both in the Japanese style of

pronunciation (the '*kun*' reading) as well as a number of possibilities in the Chinese style (the '*on*' reading).

At the time Sōseki was writing, the modern language was in the process of becoming established, and it was customary to hesitate over one's choice of Chinese characters, as there were several which could be suitable for the transcription of one and the same word. This was the situation of the purser Saji in his search for a more 'conceptual' character that would not smack excessively of the concrete or mundane, believing as he did that a well-known author would be able to guide him without difficulty. The uncertainty felt by Sōseki, whether fictional or historical, is representative of the linguistic situation of the period.

15 '*Kana*' in the Japanese text. As mentioned above, '*hiragana*' enables any Japanese word to be transcribed phonetically. Modern Japanese tends more and more away from difficult Chinese characters (*kanji*) and towards a preference for such *hiragana* transcription. However, to purists or traditionalists (like Saji), this change represents both an aesthetic and a cultural impoverishment. For a description of the fictional quality also involved in Sōseki's socially awkward response to the purser, see the Introduction.

16 In Tokyo, in the Southwest of Iidabashi quarter (Chiyoda-Ku), adjacent to the Imperial Palace and along the Kanda River, a stone wharf had been built for the loading and unloading of merchandise.

17 Sōseki frequently uses the term 'coolie', or *kūrī*, which derives from a name for low-paid, native workers used by Europeans in India and Asia. In using this term, Sōseki invokes a parallel between the colonizing Europeans and the Japanese presence in Manchuria. See the Introduction for a discussion of Sōseki's use of these and other pejorative terms.

18 The term '*rōsuke*' used here is the phonetic equivalent of 'Russki', used in a mockingly pejorative sense in the aftermath of the Russo-Japanese War (1904–5).

19 '*Chan*' in Japanese: another pejorative term for the Chinese. The term fell into disuse after the Second World War. Critics have speculated whether Sōseki used such words to appeal to the nationalist temper of the newspaper readership in the time following the Russo-Japanese War. See the Introduction.

20 A small village at the end of the nineteenth century, Harbin grew when it was reached by the railway junction with the Manchouli-Vladivostock line which allowed continuous travel from Harbin to Dairen and, above all, to Beijing. Harbin was also known for the quality of its horses. It grew from 40,000 inhabitants in 1911 to 750,000 in 1942.

21 The *tatami* is a padded straw mat measuring 1.82 by 0.91 metres in area and a half centimetre in thickness, with a dark border running along the two long sides. *Tatami* mats cover most rooms in traditional Japanese houses, particularly the reception rooms and bedrooms. Because of its standardized size, it is also used as a unit for calculating the area of the rooms in homes or apartments today.

22 Sōseki, in other words, is standing on the open mezzanine level of this grand room.

23 A dwarf tree grown in a pot for aesthetic purposes and produced by atrophying the roots and tying up the stems and branches to control their growth.

24 One branch of the SMR had installed its Tokyo offices in the Manihana quarter – in the present district of Minato-ku.

25 Shimpei Gōtō (1857–1929) was a Japanese count and politician, who functioned (sequentially) as Governor of Formosa, Minister of the Interior, Minister of Foreign Affairs, and Mayor of Tokyo, as well as being the first President of the SMR. See Introduction for a description of his political intent for the SMR.

26 This is the Emperor of China, Gong Xu, who reigned from 1875–1909 and who belonged to the Manchu Qing dynasty (1644–1911).

27 Such scenes of social awkwardness are reminiscent of much of Sōseki's early literary works, where the naïve young hero continually finds himself in socially compromising positions.

28 A light cotton *kimono* worn indoors year round and outdoors in the summer. While the Japanese are less likely to wear the *kimono* except for formal or official functions (such as graduation ceremonies, coming of age ceremonies, and tea ceremonies), the *yukata* is frequently worn by both sexes in summer, when the whole family attends village or district festivals. On these occasions, young girls wear particularly brightly coloured *yukata*.

29 This hotel, situated in Dairen, was considered a luxury hotel and had the advantage of offering two types of accommodation: Western and Japanese.

30 Lushun or Liu Chouen in Chinese, Ryûjun in Japanese. A Southern Manchurian port situated at the end of the Liaodong peninsula, near Dairen. It formed the subject of the rivalry between the Japanese, who occupied it in 1894–95 (at the time of the Sino-Japanese War) and the Russians (who from 1898 onwards built an important naval base there, seized by the Japanese in 1904–05).

31 A coal-mining town situated near Fukuoka, in the north of the Island of Kyūshū, where Sōseki taught in two schools after leaving Tokyo.

32 Below, Sōseki actually visits Fushun and learns of its abundance of coal, although the narrative also breaks off suddenly just as we enter a mine.

33 This scene is suggestive of international tensions within Asia. See Introduction for information on why it would cause Sōseki considerable anxiety to be considered Korean or Chinese.

34 See an account of this episode in Sōseki's *Tower of London*.

35 *Hakama* and *haori* are traditional Japanese men's garments: the former resembling trousers with wide legs and ample folds, and the latter fitting the upper body, but cut full and short with a folded front similar to a *kimono*.

36 Nakamura Zekō, Sōseki's high school friend, became the second President of the SMR. He was also known for his rough, country manners, according to Joshua Fogel. Sōseki makes constant comparisons in this travelogue between Zekō's rusticated ways and his own, more cosmopolitan understanding.

37 The club was located opposite the Hotel Yamato.

38 Literally 'the Bridge of Japan', a reinforced concrete bridge situated on the Oyama Boulevard, running from the north side of the main square in Dairen. It overhung an access road that served the landing stage of the SMR. The name is reminiscent of bridges found in Tokyo and Osaka. In Edo, the Nihonbashi bridge marked the point from which all distances were measured, making it even more symbolic of Japanese national pride.

39 A game similar to chess, of Chinese origin. The pieces are distinguished both by their shape and by the Chinese characters inscribed on them.

40 Sōseki here uses Zekō's inability to speak English as a token of his lack of worldly sophistication. It is odd that Sōseki, whose English skills must have been unsurpassed by other Japanese at the time, does not speak English

himself at such times, and refuses to speak to Westerners in English during the travelogue, with only one exception. See Chapter 12 and the Introduction for more on Sōseki's complicated relationship with the West.

41 'Proposed by', and 'Seconded by' are in English (Roman alphabet) in the original text. This scene clarifies the role of English in Japanese Meiji culture, particularly the combination of prestige and nationalism it invoked. See Introduction for further discussion of Sōseki's ambivalence about his mastery of the English language. The Club's name (literally 'red beard') has less to do with pirates than with Japanese accounts of the first visits of the Dutch to Japan, particularly a fascination with their red hair – a hair colour that in Japan had traditionally been associated with other-worldly spirits. The empty Japanese club built in conspicuously Western style may also have symbolic meaning for Japan's attempt to become a grand Western power through its manipulation of Manchuria (see Introduction). Of particular interest is Zekō's simultaneous desire to seem cosmopolitan (the Club is 'dull' when there are no foreigners there) and to remain in Japan (his statement that he accepted his position on the condition that he would not have to live abroad).

42 A covered carriage, drawn by one horse.

43 This is presumably the tower mentioned in Chapter 6: 'A high narrow tower rose from the centre of the roof of Zekō's villa, blackening part of the deep blue, almost violet, sky.'

44 The amusement park of Dairen, called 'Electricity Park', was served by the electric railway and situated to the west of the city, on Fushimi Hill. It offered visitors a wide variety of electrically operated installations, which was quite rare at the time. This park impressed Sōseki enough for him to return to it in one of his novels, *After the Departed*. A statue of Komura Jutarō (1855–1911), politician and Minister of Foreign Affairs after the Russo-Japanese War, was erected in the park. Thereafter it was called 'Komura Park'.

45 See the Introduction for more on the cultural role of the SMR.

46 In this, the second scene revolving around embarrassment caused by Chinese characters, Zekō refers to the *kanji* characters for amusement (*koraku*) which literally mean 'public play' or 'public amusement'.

47 In this and many succeeding chapters, Sōseki jumps to a new location, only gradually revealing it to the reader in the course of the chapter. See the Introduction for part of the reason behind this disjointed narrative technique.

48 Colza oil, also known as rapeseed oil, was produced in Manchuria by the SMR as a commercial export. See Young for a discussion of the vast SMR industrial and agricultural research projects.

49 Takamine Jōkichi: a chemist, specializing in pharmacology (1855–1955). These passages are filled with puns on 'refined' versus 'unrefined' materials, whether colza oil, saké, or pottery. One implication seems to be that the Japanese 'refined' the crude materials of Manchuria.

50 In the text, this is five to six *chō*. A *chō* was an old unit of measurement approximately equivalent to 109.9 metres.

51 '*Gemu*', or '*Zemu*', is a Japanese medication that Sōseki also mentions in his novel *Light and Darkness*. It was used in the late Meiji to early Taisho period to clean the mouth. In larger doses, it was thought to help the digestion and the appetite. The same company (Aikokudō) still makes a similar product, now called '*Jintan*'.

52 In the original text, he is called *Masakikō*, or 'Marquis Masaki'. *Kō* is a suffix of courtesy expressing membership of the nobility. As we shall see farther on, this is Masaki Tachibana.

53 Robert Hart (1843–1911), a British diplomat posted to various towns in China.
54 This is the prestigious Tokyo Imperial University, now called the University of Tokyo (or *Tōdai*).
55 An ancient fief governed by an overlord until the Meiji era, which commenced in 1868.
56 This fief of Yanagawa was situated to the south of the old province of Chikugo, now the Fukuoka department (to the north of the Island of Kyushu on the other side of the Shimonoseki Strait).
57 Literally, '*Tanaka-kun*'. The particle *-kun* is used when a man is addressing a younger man in a certain social situations (such as within a commercial concern, in a position of public authority, or in a teaching establishment).
58 Natsume Sōseki began his literary career in 1905 by publishing *I am a Cat* ·(*Wagahai wa neko de aru*). From January onwards, it appeared serially in the journal *Hototogisu* (*The Cuckoo*) – a journal that united around the great poet Masaoka Shiki and appealed to those who wanted to revive the tradition of the *haiku*. The narrator is a cat – alternately wise, mocking, facetious, and impudent. See the Introduction for further information on Sōseki's publishing career.
59 A town situated in the south of the Department of Fukuoka (to the north of the Island of Kyushu), washed by the Chikugo River. Its present population is 220,000.
60 An old province corresponding to the South of the Department of Fukuoka.
61 A town situated to the Northeast of the Department of Saga (Kyūshu). In former times, it was a strategic harbour. Its present population is 80,000.
62 An old province corresponding to the Department of Saga and to the Department of Nagasaki.
63 Fushun, or Fou Zhouen, a town in the Liaoning region of China, to the east of Shenyang, was well-known for its coal and oil shale. It now has a population of over 1,000,000.
64 Kitagawa Utamaro (1753–1806). One of the most famous masters of Japanese woodblock printing (*ukiyōe*). One of Utamaro's specialties was the portraiture of women. He developed a highly characteristic style of portraits of women with large facial features. Among his most significant works are 'Ten studies of feminine physiognomy', 'Two types of feminine face', and 'Twelve hours in the pleasure quarters'.
65 This is the author's real first name, Sōseki being a pen name. See Introduction.
66 Zekō's one-word overture is first rendered in Roman alphabet within the text, and then in katakana, to emphasize his faulty pronunciation of the word. See note 14 above.
67 An island, well known for tourism and recreation, situated Southwest of Tokyo, in the *Kanagawa* department.
68 *Sen* is an old monetary unit: one *yen* was equivalent to one hundred *sen*.
69 This is a member of a firm whose primary function is to organize social events, such as meals in restaurants, or visits to the bar, and who settles the bill on behalf of the company (*shujinyaku*).
70 This is a reference to a private prep school named Kōtō Gijuku that Sōseki attended in 1883.
71 *Shiruko*, a sweet purée made from little red beans (*azuki*).
72 Okayama: a region of Japan situated between Hiroshima and Osaka. 'Sago' is an abbreviated form of the first name Sagoro. It is possible that there is additional ridicule in an intended pun with a homonym: '*sago*' also means monkey-child.

73 The most northern of the Japanese islands, Hokkaidō is separated from Honshū, the main island, by the Strait of Tsugara. Its area is 78,152 square kilometres, and its population is 5,576,000. A mountainous, tree-covered island with vigorous agriculture (stockbreeding), it was the last island in Japan to benefit from modern civilization and still performs a pioneering function in a certain number of spheres. Its main towns are Sapporo, Hokodate, Muroran, Kushiro, and Otaru. The island has long, cold winters (the temperature falling below 20° C) and hot, damp summers.

74 The English words 'very, very!' are here rendered in *katakana* phoneticized alphabet to emphasize the inadequately inauthentic pronunciation (according to Sōseki's perspective).

75 Haga Yaichi (1867–1927) was a specialist in Japanese literature and also a professor at the Imperial University of Tokyo.

76 In the Japanese system of marking, 60 is the passing score out of 100, corresponding to 10 out of 20 in France, for example.

77 Fogel and others have observed that part of Zekō's motive in inviting Sōseki on this tour was publicity for the SMR in the *Asahi* newspaper. Sōseki allowed the SMR to pay many of his expenses, yet struggled to remain objective, rather than to serve for company public relations. See Introduction for a discussion of Sōseki's political stance as narrator.

78 This is '*Tūzoku kanso gundan*,' published in 1695 (Genroku 7).

79 Sōseki makes frequent reference to the dangerous conditions under which the Chinese workers lived and worked. See Introduction for the high rates of death among Chinese workers associated with the SMR.

80 Sun-dried globefish.

81 The traditional Manchu masculine hair style. When the Manchu (Qing) dynasty came to power in China, it became obligatory. It was prohibited by the People's Republic.

82 In Sōseki's time, Japanese-style walls were made of timber, and thick walls made of brick were considered 'Western'.

83 One had to step slightly down at the entry way to Japanese-style rooms carpeted with *tatami* mats.

84 This may be one of the earliest references to Mahjong, the Chinese game of chance for four players, which was very popular in the Qing Dynasty. It was not introduced to Japan and to Europe until the 1920s.

85 One of the two leading Japanese industrial groups, called '*Zaibatsu*'. In the seventeenth century, its headquarters near Tokyo already employed over 1000 people. In the Meiji Era (1868–1912), while Japan was experiencing rapid industrialization, the Mitsui family urged the state to open mines, shipyards, spinning mills, and factories and then bought the plants. The wars against China (1894–5) and Russia (1904–5) led to their further rapid expansion. The Mitsui were soon to control the country's entire engineering industry.

86 This is a reference to Sir Robert Harry Inglis Palgrave (1827–1919), English banker and economist, publisher of the *Economist*. In addition to works on the bank and on the taxation system, he published a *Dictionary of Economics* in three volumes (1894–99).

87 A popular form of public entertainment was listening to storytellers of various sorts: '*Rakugo*', '*Kōdan*' (dramatic narration of historical events by a '*Kōdan-shi*'), '*Manzai*' (dialogues), '*Rōkyoku*' of the '*Naniwabu-shi*', jugglers, lecturers, concerts and other variety performances. The '*Yose*' appeared at the beginning of the Edo epoch.

88 Natsume Sōseki also gained prominence as a lecturer, whose lectures were among the most important of the period. By 1909, at the time when he

wrote this account, he had already given a lecture on 'The Philosophical Foundations of Literature' ('*Bungei no tetsugakuteki kisō*') and 'The Behaviour of the Creative Writer' ('*Sōsakka no taido*'). In August 1911, he gave a series of four remarkable lectures dealing in particular with individual liberty: 'Entertainment and Professional Activity' ('*Dōraku to shokugyō*'), 'Modern Japanese Civilization' ('*Gendai nihon no kaika*'), 'Content and Form' ('*Nakami to keishiki*') and 'Literature and Morality' ('*Bungei to dōtoku*'). In 1914, 'My Conception of the Individual' ('*Watakushino kōjinshugi*') appeared, synthesizing many of the ideas in these lectures.

89 A region to the Southwest of the archipelago, in the Island of Kyushu, between the towns of Nagasaki and Kagoshima, on the East China Sea coast, which faces the Island of Ryukyu (Okinawa) and Formosa. The fief of Satsuma, in competition with the neighbouring fiefdom of Chōshu, played a decisive part in the historical struggle for power from 1860 onwards, destroying the Shōgun institution and leading to the 'Imperial Restoration', pronounced by the fiefs of Satsuma and Chōshu in January 1868.

90 A quarter situated to the northwest of the district of *Chiyoka-ku* in Tokyo. In the Edo era, it housed the dwellings of the vassals of the shōgun (Hatamoto).

91 At the time of the civil war that set Japan ablaze in 1868.

92 Wooden sandals with boards as soles and supported by two small vertical slats for traction and elevation. Straps known as '*hanao*' secure them to the foot.

93 Straw sandals (*waraji*) secured to the foot by two cords. The cords are fastened to the sandal between the big toe and the other toes, wrap around the heel, and then are tied together above the instep. These sandals were generally used for travelling.

94 In the traditional Japanese home, this is the area between the floored and the raised sections, where one receives and takes leave of guests (*shikidai*).

95 '*Kansuzume*' has a number of associations for Japanese, including a particularly good kind of *yakitori*. The nickname here, however, is based on the appearance of sparrows in the winter – namely, how they ruffle their feathers to keep warm, sticking them out perpendicular to their bodies and letting them be blown to and fro by the wind, like the few hairs sticking out from Satō's head.

96 The torpedoing of three Russian ships at Port Arthur by the Japanese on 8 February 1904 marked the outbreak of the Russo-Japanese War. It was at least partially provoked by the disappointment of the Japanese Government at the intervention of the European powers, who intended to limit the advantages derived from Japan's victory over China in 1895. (Germans were installed in the Bay of Jiaozhou, the French in Guangshouwan, and the Russians in Liaodong and in Korea.) While the blockade was maintained by the Japanese fleet, General Stoessel's Russian garrison was besieged by Generals Oku and Nogi. After unsuccessful attempts by the Russian squadron to break out on 10 April (on the death of Admiral Makarov) and on 10 August, the sailors still defended the site. But on 15 December, the capture of Hill 203, which dominated the trade route, forced the squadron to disperse. The garrison surrendered on 2 January 1905, after a resistance that cost the Japanese more than 50,000 men. See the Introduction for further information.

97 Literally, the 'Region of the Northern Marches'.

98 Mount Hakugyoku (120 metres high) separated the old town from the new town of Port Arthur. This Mount, held by the Russian Army during the Russo-Japanese War, was also the site of violent combat.

99 The Hyōchu Tower, sixty-six metres high, was built as a memorial to the 16,044 Japanese soldiers and officers who died in the battle.

100 Mount Keikan, situated in the Northwest of the old town, was likewise the scene of violent and bloody battles.

101 See Introduction for an explanation of Sōseki's emphasis on his poor memory, particularly striking when he recounts his experience at the patriotic sites commemorating the recent Russo-Japanese War. The exact details of these adventures would have been of extreme interest to his readers, many of whom must have been frustrated by Sōseki's (fictional?) forgetfulness.

102 This must be a reference to General Kondrachenko, who was killed at Port Arthur in December 1904.

103 See Introduction for an explanation of Sōseki's tendency to end chapters with vistas, a tendency that increases as *Travels* proceeds.

104 Sapporo, the chief town of the island province of Hokkaidō, had an approximate population of 1,500,000 at this period, and served as a centre of communications networks, administration, industry, and commerce. Hashimoto taught at the University of Sapporo.

105 This must designate the Bay of Port Arthur, reflecting like a mirror beneath the sun, c.f. 'The harbour of Port Arthur, smooth as a mirror, shone dark green . . .' (Chapter 22).

106 During the naval siege at Port Arthur, General Nogi suffered embarrassing losses – 69,000 out of 120,000 troops. The embarrassing failure ultimately helped cause General Nogi's dramatic self-immolation after the death of Emperor Meiji – an event that becomes an important part of the plot of Sōseki's novel *Kokoro*.

107 This was the tactic used by the Japanese Army to block Russian warships from leaving the Port Arthur harbour.

108 An English inch (2.54cm); the cables were 18cm wide.

109 A kind of stew, very popular from the Meiji era (1868–1912) onwards, made of sliced beef cooked with vegetables and soybean paste (*tofu*) in a sweetened soy sauce. The popularity of this dish marked the beginning of the general consumption of meat in Japan.

110 The term 'New Town' was used in SMR propaganda to indicate the refinement and transformation of Manchuria under Japanese influence. Photographs of the 'new towns' in books such as *Modern Manchuria*, for example, juxtapose illustrations of 'swampy areas' with photographs of expansive buildings with Western architecture (c.f. Kinney, 28).

111 Round, smooth, pebble-shaped pieces used in the chess-like game of *Go*.

112 Masaoka Shiki (1871–1902), a modern Japanese poet and contemporary of Natsume Sōseki. At a very early stage, he showed interest in traditional poetic forms inherited from classical Chinese (*kanshi*), such as *waka* and *haiku*, and decided to revive the *haiku* style, which had become obsolescent. In 1897, friends created for him the well-known literary review *Hototogisu* (*The Cuckoo*). Natsume Sōseki, who was indebted to him for his initiation to *haiku*, published his first work of prose fiction, *I am a Cat,* in *Hototogisu* in 1905.

113 Ōmiya Park, in northern Tokyo.

114 A card worn behind to keep traditional trousers, or *hakama,* hanging straight (*koshi ita*).

115 This is Sōseki's friend Satō Tomukuma.

116 Strong rectangular paper designed to support calligraphy (*Tanzaku*). Originally, these thick paper streamers bore coloured designs on a gold-speckled background, according to the month of the year. They generally measure thirty centimetres by six. On each fresh flowering, it was the

custom to inscribe streamers with appropriate verses and suspend them from branches of the tree.

117 A poem composed according to the '*haiku*' form (three lines of 5, 7, and 5 syllables in length).

118 Satō, whom Sōseki calls an expert in calligraphy, mistakes one character for another when reading the text: namely, he mistakes the cursive form of *te* (hand) for *toshi* (year).

119 '*Toro*' is an abbreviation for '*Torokko*', which is the *katakana*, phonetic rendition of the English word 'truck'. *Torokko* means either truck or trolley in Japanese.

120 Sōseki uses the term '*Asagao*', referring to the morning glory or convolvulus (*pharbitis hederacea*).

121 A fish similar to a small trout (*Plecoglossus altivelis*). It is very popular in Japan, and it is not surprising that Sōseki, despite his stomach pains, wishes to obtain some.

122 See note 91.

123 The hot spring, or outdoor thermal spa, is very important to the Japanese people and their culture. This also applies to Sōseki and his literary characters. For example, the hero of the novel *Pillow of Grass* deliberately chooses a hot spring as a place in which to sojourn and create. This is not only owing to the therapeutic properties of the water, but also because the very expression 'thermal spa' (*onsen*) gives him a certain feeling of gaiety: 'I am content to think of the verse by Po kiu yu: "The hot spring, the water is smooth, cleanses the oily skin." As soon as I hear the expression "thermal spa", I feel a certain gaiety, as expressed in this verse. I consider that a thermal spring that fails to awaken this feeling is unworthy of its name. And I ask from the thermal spa nothing more than this idea.' For the hero, the bath has a specific function – namely, that of snatching him away from the rhythm of time, of causing him to leave this world down below and to rise aloft. The vapours that, on a spring evening, rise from the thermal springs, gently enveloping the bather, enable him to believe that he is in another time. Floating, one escapes the suffering of life. To abandon one's floating soul to the current, is this not more pleasurable than to become a disciple of Christ? These statements give clear evidence of a conception of the 'transcendental' role played by the hot spring in Japan.

124 For the metaphor, Sōseki here uses the term '*kaimaki*', a traditional padded night garment with sleeves and often bearing printed designs.

125 The reason for embarrassment and ridicule here was the simple reason that the water, contrary to appearances, was actually boiling.

126 This is a reference to the Southern School of Chinese Song painting, generally featuring steep mountains in dark hues, and tending towards impressionism, abstraction, and minimalism, in contrast to the Northern School's tendency towards realism. The Northern school was connected with academicians, while the Southern School was connected with literati instead. It is befitting that Sōseki's preference would be for the Southern, more expressionistic School.

127 '*Matsuyama*' in Japanese, a mountain covered with pine trees.

128 Asukayama Hill is situated in the northern part of Tokyo (*Kita-ku* district). It is celebrated for its cherry blossoms (*sakura*) and became a public park in 1873.

129 If Natsume Sōseki did not understand spoken Chinese, as he states several times in this text, he nonetheless showed a remarkable knowledge of classical written Chinese. It should be remembered that he very frequently

composed '*kanshi*', Chinese poems, and was considered by many to be the greatest *kanshi* artist in modern Japan.

130 *The Tale of the Three Kingdoms* (*Sanguo ji yanyi*) was a very popular story written in China at the end of the Yuan period (1280–1369) or at the beginning of the Ming period (1368–1644), and attributed to Luo Guanzhong (1330?–1400?). The 'Three Kingdoms' refers to the three sections into which China was divided from 222 to 265, the kingdoms of Shu, Wei, and Wu. By the end of Ming (1644), *Three Kingdoms* had appeared in twenty editions, and its characters eventually became as familiar to nineteenth and twentieth-century Chinese audiences as Shakespeare's to the English. It was repeatedly transformed into theatre plays in China and Japan, and often formed a source of art motifs for woodblock print artists, such as Hokusai. Since Sōseki is presumably referring to a Meiji version of the text, it could well have included illustrations by Hokusai, as suggested by the passage below (Chapter 47). See note 162.

131 Poems of 17 syllables, in three lines of 5, 7 and 5 syllables respectively. *Haiku* are still a highly favoured form of political inspiration and commentary. See Chapters 30 and 37 for examples.

132 A thick oblong card or board intended for a commemorative piece of calligraphy, such as a poem or a motto.

133 The writer does not name any town here. Natsume Sōseki's diary, or '*Nikki*', however, indicates that he left the Xiong Yue Zheng Spa at 4 pm and arrived at Ying Gou, a harbour town situated at the mouth of the Liao River, by 8 pm.

134 Futabatei Shimei (1864–1909) was a Japanese novelist, who specialized in Russian literature. Appointed as the Moscow correspondent of the *Asahi* newspaper, he died in the Gulf of Bengal on the way back to Japan. We are indebted to him not only for some remarkable translations, such as that of Turgenev's *On the Eve*, but also for the first Japanese novel written in the spoken language (often called Japan's first 'modern novel') *Ukigumo* (*Floating Clouds*). Shimei himself gives an account of his treatment at the Russian harbour, the incident to which this passage refers: 'On 7 June 1902, Futabatei Shimei departed Vladivostock for Harbin to work with Tokunaga Shoten. At the border station, Futabatei Shimei gave Mr Kanegai (a member of Tokunaga Shoten's staff) 25 Rubles to buy two 2nd class tickets to Harbin. At the gate, the Russian clerk took the 25 Rubles, but insisted that they were still 4 Rubles short. Then Mr Kanegai took four Rubles from Mr Hayashia (another member of Tokunaga Shoten's staff) and handed over 4 Rubles to the clerk, expecting to receive the tickets. However, the Russian clerk then claimed he had not yet received the initial 25 Rubles. Mr Kanegai was astonished with the Russian attitude and lost his words. It was close to the departure time, so Futabatei Shimei paid the additional 25 Rubles for the tickets to Harbin. They were cheated and got to pay the fare twice.'

135 One of the main temples of Tokyo, dedicated to Kannon and situated in Asakusa, a popular quarter of Northwest Tokyo, near the famous River Sumioda.

136 This beam (*Agari gamachi*) is provided in the traditional Japanese home as a simple means of ascending from the hard-packed floor of the hall (*doma*) to the raised level of the other rooms.

137 The fifty bamboo divining rods traditionally used by fortune-tellers (*zeichiku*) in Japan.

138 Literally 'zigzag bridge' cakes, referring to their shape.

139 The Liao He River flows into the Gulf of Bohai, near Ying Kō; it is 1456 km long.

140 Bay or Gulf of Bohai, the former Gulf of Petchili: a large gulf of the Yellow Sea, formed by the rocky peninsula of Liaodong to the north and Shandong to the south, opening towards the great plain of North China and the central lowlands of Northeast China. The Bay of Bohai contains many rich oil deposits.

141 From the Chinese '*sanpan*', which means three planks. A flat-bottomed Asian vessel propelled by sculls, oars and sails. It has a plaited bamboo dome in the centre as a shelter for the passengers.

142 Ying Kō is a Manchurian harbour town on the Gulf of Bohai at the mouth of the Liao He River. Ying Kō is now a commercial and industrial centre with a population of 200,000.

143 A harbour town on the Tsushima Strait opposite Japan, Busan is now the second largest city and the main port of South Korea. It has 3,200,000 inhabitants and has become a diversified industrial centre.

144 Literally 'Colonized Company' ('*takushoku kaisha*').

145 Andong is a port situated in the Liaoning region, at the mouth of the River Yelu, near the Korean frontier. The town now has a population of 420,000. Its major industries are textile, iron, steel, and papers.

146 This passage is interesting, given that two years later, in 1911, Sōseki rejected the Japanese government's offer of an honorary doctorate degree (*bungaku hakase*). See Rubin, 26.

147 The railway line is raised by comparison with the plain and constructed along a kind of dike, so that it will not be submerged in the event of floods.

148 Wei Shuzi (1624–1680), was a Chinese writer who lived at the beginning of the Qing Dynasty. His works appeared in Japan in the Meiji era, at the end of the 1870s, and were used as entrance examination subjects at the army's military academy.

149 This refers to a dish consisting of *tofu* cut up into cubes and served with a little soy sauce.

150 The thermal spa of Tang Kang Zu was just after the eleventh stop on the railway line travelling from Xiong Yue Zheng and the tenth travelling from Mukden. The baths are 400 metres Northwest of the station.

151 The period immediately following the Japanese invasion of part of Manchuria after the Russo-Japanese War.

152 Mukden, now Shen Yang, was founded on the Hun He River, a tributary of the Liao He. It was overtaken by Manchus in 1625, and named Mukden (Mukhden). The Manchus built an imperial palace there, as well as two imperial burial mounds: that of Qing Daizong, founder of the Qing Dynasty, and that of his grandfather. In February and March 1905, it was the locus of the main battle of the Russo-Japanese War. It now has over 4,500,000 inhabitants and is the third largest Chinese city, after Shanghai and Beijing.

153 Rokkotsu was a famous Japanese *haiku* poet (1870–1944), as well as a disciple of Masaoka Shiki. He enlisted in the army and was wounded on the battlefields in the Sino-Japanese War (1894–95).

154 A place situated 60 km northwest of Mukden, containing an imperial tomb from the Shin Dynasty.

155 A term used in the Meiji Era for Japanese returning from sojourns in Europe – and by extension for all novelties with Western associations. In current usage, it also refers to the snobbery of a certain category of inhabitants of Tokyo.

156 Hai Zheng is the second stop after the thermal spa of Tan Kang Zu, travelling towards Mukden.

157 Little bells known as '*furin*', suspended from a roof canopy. They emit a pleasant tinkling sound in the breeze on hot summer days and produce a psychological impression of freshness.

158 Sōseki is considered one of the modern Japanese masters of Chinese poetry (*kanshi*).

159 The '*furoshiki*', a traditional square of fabric, sometimes pleasingly dyed and ornamented, is still quite commonly used in Japan for wrapping and conveying objects.

160 This refers to Emperor Keiko (71–130).

161 Natsume Sōseki, when writing this passage, appears to suspect that the cooking might also have been done with the waste water from the bath.

162 Hokusai Katsushika, a Japanese painter and woodblock print designer (1760–1849). He produced a monumental and richly varied oeuvre. *Tale of the Three Kingdoms, attributed to* Luo Guanzhong (1330?–1400?), had frequently been re-published in Japan. Editions in late Edo and Meiji frequently contained illustrations by Hokusai.

163 As the reader will understand by the end of the chapter, the offices of the SMR are installed in this traditional Chinese home.

164 A painting, engraving or piece of calligraphy suspended vertically.

165 See note 2 above on the cosmopolitan significance of Kanda, and therefore for clarification of the humour in this passage.

166 Animal's coats, of course, generally lose their gloss at the beginning of Autumn, as the winter fur thickens. The suggestion is that the Manchurian sun is so strong that it counteracts this natural thickening of the fur.

167 Literally 'move the shafts and the packsaddle in alteration' ('*geri tari, getsu tari*'), thus expressing the left-to-right and front-to-back movements that the vehicle was made to perform – and which caused some feeling of sickness on the part of the passengers.

168 An English art journal assiduously read by Natsume Sōseki.

169 See Introduction for a discussion of Sōseki's difficult stay in London and his ambivalence over his excellent proficiency in spoken and written English.

170 A portable tin-plate mining lamp (*Kantelō*, from the Dutch 'Kandelaar'), featuring a wick and operated with petroleum or vegetable oil. They were used in the Japanese mines from the Edo epoch onwards. In the novel *The Miner*, published in 1908, Natsume Sōseki expressed his admiration of the efficiency of these lamps, claiming that they would practically never go out.

171 This chapter appeared on 31 December 1909. Despite the fact that he had all the material available for writing the continuation, Sōseki ended his travel narrative here. According to the Iwanami Publishing House, it seemed strange to continue the following year on the same subject. The sudden interruption of this work seems particularly strange, given that it occurs just as Sōseki visits the mining town of Fushun. Sōseki develops his interest in the mining motif in his novel *The Miner*. See Introduction for further suggestions on the sudden ending of the narrative.

Select Bibliography

Andō, Hikotarō. *Mantetsu, Nihon teikokushugi to Chūgoku.* Tokyo: Ochanomizu shobō, 1965.

Aoyagi, Tatsuo. *Nakamura Zeko and Natsume Sōseki.* Bensei-Sha, 1996.

Ara, Masato. *Sōseki bungaku zenshū.* Tokyo: Shūeisha, 1974.

Beongcheon, Yu. *Natsume Sōseki.* New York: Twayne Publishers, 1969.

Brodey, Inger Sigrun. 'Natsume Sōseki and Laurence Sterne: Cross-Cultural Discourse on Literary Linearity.' *Comparative Literature* 50:3 (1998): 193–219.

——. '*Kokoro*, Sensibility, and the Language of Feeling: on the Associationist Aesthetics of Natsume Sōseki.' *Studies on Voltaire and the Eighteenth Century* (1996): 1226–1227.

Doi, Takeo. *The Psychological World of Natsume Sōseki.* Trans. William J. Tyler. London: Harvard University East Asian Research Center, 1976.

Duus, Peter, Ramon H. Myers, and Mark R. Peattie, eds. *The Japanese Informal Empire in China, 1895–1937.* Princeton: Princeton University Press, 1989.

Etō, Jun. 'Natsume Sōseki: A Japanese Meiji Intellectual.' *The American Scholar* 34 (1965): 603–619.

Fogel, Joshua A. 'Japanese Literary Travelers in Prewar China.' *Harvard Journal of Asiatic Studies* 49 (1989): 575–602.

——. *The Literature of Travel in the Japanese Rediscovery of China: 1862–1945.* Stanford: Stanford University Press, 1996.

Fowler, Edward. *The Rhetoric of Confession: Shishōsetsu in Early Twentieth-Century Japanese Fiction.* Berkeley: University of California Press, 1988.

Fujii, James A. 'Contesting the Meiji Subject: Sōseki's *Neko* Reconsidered.' *Harvard Journal of Asiatic Studies* 49 (1989): 553–574.

——. 'Writing Out Asia: Modernity, Canon, and Natsume Sōseki's *Kokoro*.' *Cultural Institutions of the Novel.* Eds. Deidre Lynch and William B. Warner. Durham: Duke University Press, 1996.

Fujitani, Takashi. 'Inventing, Forgetting, Remembering: Toward a Historical Ethnography of the Nation-State,' *Cultural Nationalism in East Asia.* Ed. Harumi Befu. Berkeley: Institute of East Asian Studies, 1993.

Fussell, Paul. *Abroad: British Literary Traveling Between the Wars.* New York: Oxford University Press, 1980.

Gessel, Van C. *Three Modern Novelists: Sōseki, Tanizaki, Kawabata.* Tokyo: Kodansha International, 1993.

Harada, Katsumasa. *Mantetsu.* Tokyo: Iwanami Shoten, 1984.

Hirakawa, Sukehiro. 'Image of a British Scholar: Natsume Sōseki's Reminiscences of his London Days,' *Proceedings of the British Association for Japanese Studies.* University of Sheffield (1980): 167–176.

Hirakawa, Sukehiro, ed. *Rediscovering Lafcadio Hearn: Japanese Legends, Life and Culture.* Folkestone: Global Oriental, 1997.

Hirota, Kōzō. *Mantetsu no shūen to sono go: aru Chūō Shikenjōin no hōkoku.* Tokyo: Seigensha, 1990.

Itō, Takeo. *Life Along the South Manchurian Railway: The Memoirs of Itō Takeo.* Trans. Joshua A. Fogel. Armonk: M.E. Sharpe, 1988.

Karatani, Kōjin. *Ifu suru ningen*. Tokyo: Tōjusha, 1979.
Keene, Donald. *Japanese Literature: An Introduction for Western Readers*. New York: Grove Press, 1955.
——. 'Natsume Sōseki.' *Dawn to the West: Japanese Literature of the Modern Era*. New York: Holt, Rinehart, and Winston, 1984.
Kenshiro, Homma. *Natsume Sōseki: A Comparative Study*. Hirakata: Kansai University of Foreign Studies, 1990.
Kinney, Henry W. *Modern Manchuria*. Dairen: 1929.
Kobayashi, Hideo. *Mantetsu: 'chi no shūdan' no tanjō to shi*. Tokyo: Yoshikawa Kōbunkan, 1996.
Matsui, Sakuko. *Natsume Sōseki as a Critic of English Literature*. Tokyo: The Centre for East Asian Cultural Studies, 1975.
McClellan, Edwin. *Two Japanese Novelists: Sōseki and Tōson*. Chicago: University of Chicago Press, 1969.
Meech-Pekarik, Julia. *The World of the Meiji Print*. New York and Tokyo: Weatherhill, 1987.
Miner, Earl. 'On the Genesis and Development of Literary Systems, Part I,' *Critical Inquiry* (Winter, 1978): 339–53.
——. *The Japanese Tradition in British and American Literature*. Princeton: Princeton University Press, 1958.
Miyanishi, Yoshio, ed. *Mantetsu Chōsabu to Ozaki Hotsumi*. Tokyo: Aki Shobō, 1983.
Miyoshi, Yukio, ed. *Natsume Sōseki jiten*. Besshū Kokubungaku. 10 July 1990: 245–246.
Miyoshi, Masao. *Accomplices of Silence: The Modern Japanese Novel*. Berkeley: University of California Press, 1974.
Myers, Ramon H. and Mark R. Peattie, eds. *The Japanese Colonial Empire, 1895–1945*. Princeton: Princeton University Press, 1984.
Natsume, Sōseki. *And Then*. Trans. Norma Moore Field. Ann Arbor: The University of Michigan Center for Japanese Studies, 1997.
——. *Botchan*. Trans. Alan Turney. Tokyo and New York: Kodansha International, 1972.
——. *Craig Sensei*. Trans. Sammy I. Tsunematsu. London: Sōseki Museum in London, 1992.
——. *Grass on the Wayside*. Trans. Edwin McClellan. Ann Arbor: Center for Japanese Studies at the University of Michigan, 1990.
——. *I am a Cat (Wagahai wa neko de aru)*. Trans. Aiko Itō and Graeme Wilson. 3 vols. Rutland and Tokyo: Tuttle, 1976–1986.
——. *Kokoro: A Novel and Selected Essays*. Trans. Edwin McClellan and Jay Rubin. Lanham: Madison Books, 1992.
——. 'Mankan tokoro dokoro.' *Sōseki zenshū*. Ed. Sōseki Junichi. Vol. 9. Tokyo: Sōseki Zenshū Kankōkai, 1918.
——. 'My Individualism: Watakushi no Kojinshugi.' *Monumenta Nipponica* 34 (1979): 26–48.
——. *Reflections*. Trans. Maria Flutsch. London: Sōseki Museum in London, 1997.
——. *Sanshiro*. Trans. Jay Rubin. Seattle: University of Washington Press, 1977.
——. *Sōseki zenshū*. Ed. Sōseki zenshū kankōkai. 20 vols. Tokyo: 1928.
——. *The Three-Cornered World (Kusamakura)*. Trans. Alan Turney. Washington, DC: Regnery Gateway, 1988.
——. *The Tower of London*. Trans. Peter Milward and Kii Nakano. Brighton: In Print Publishing, 1992.
Nitobe, Inazo, et al. *Western Influences in Modern Japan: A Series of Papers on Cultural Relations*. Chicago: University of Chicago Press, 1931.

SELECT BIBLIOGRAPHY

Okazaki, Yoshie, ed. *Japanese Literature in the Meiji Era*. Trans. V.H. Viglielmo. Obunsha, 1955.

Rubin, Jay. 'Sōseki on Individualism.' *Monumenta Nipponica* 34 (1979): 21–25.

Sansom, G.B. *The Western World and Japan: A Study in the Interaction of European and Asiatic Cultures*. New York: Alfred A. Knopf, 1950.

Shimei, Futabatei. *Japan's First Modern Novel: 'Ukigumo'*. Trans. Marleigh Grayer Ryan. Ann Arbor: The University of Michigan, 1990.

Shively, Donald H, ed. *Tradition and Modernization in Japanese Culture*. Princeton: Princeton University Press, 1971.

South Manchuria Railway Company. *Manchuria: Land of Opportunities*. New York: Thomas F. Logan, 1922.

——. *Manshū Jihen to Mantetsu*. Ed. Minami Manshū Tetsudō Kabushiki Kaisha. Tokyo: Hara Shobō, 1974.

Takeuchi, Minoru. 'Sōseki no "Mankan tokoro dokoro".' *Nihonjin ni totte no Chūgoku zō*. Shunjūsha, 1966.

Tomoda, Etsuo. 'Natsume Sōseki to Chūgoku, Chōsen.' *Sakka no Ajia taiken: Kindai Nihon bungaku no inga*. Ed. Ashiya Nobukazu, Ueda Hiroshi, and Kimura Kazuaki. Tokyo: Sekai Shisōsha, 1992.

Tsukamoto, Toshiaki. 'Sōseki: His Scholar-Critic Years (1890–1909)' in Iijima, Takehisa and Vardaman, James M. eds. *The World of Natsume Sōseki*. Japan: Kinseido Ltd., (1987): 17–52.

Ueda, Makoto. *Modern Japanese Writers and the Nature of Literature*. Stanford: Stanford University Press, 1976.

Walker, Janet. 'The Cramped Room in the City: A Setting for the Nineteenth-Century Individualist.' Ed. Roger Bauer. *Proceedings of the International Comparative Literature Association* (1990): 288–293.

——. 'The Fusion of Japanese and Western Poetic Systems in Two Works of Modern Japanese Fiction.' *Proceedings of the Xth Congress of the International Comparative Literature Association* (1985): 681–686.

——. *The Japanese Novel of the Meiji Period and the Ideal of Individualism*. Princeton: Princeton University Press, 1979.

Wilson, George M. *Patriots and Redeemers in Japan: Motives in the Meiji Restoration*. Chicago: University of Chicago Press, 1992.

Yiu, Angela. *Chaos and Order in the Works of Natsume Sōseki*. Honolulu: University of Hawaii Press, 1998.

Yoneda, Toshiaki. 'Sōseki no Mankan ryokō.' *Bungaku* 40.9 (1972): 62–74.

Young, John. *The Research Activities of the South Manchurian Railway Company, 1907–1945: A History and Bibliography*. New York: Columbia University, 1966.

Chronology

Events in Sōseki's Life

1853 – Admiral Perry's first visit to Japan followed by opening of Japanese ports and the end of the era of seclusion.

1867 – Natsume Kinnosuke – better known by his pen name Sōseki – born February 9, Edo (Tokyo), Japan. Soon put out to nurse.

1868 – Adopted into the Shiobara family. Meiji Era begins; Emperor Meiji's 5-Point Plan.

1874–1878 – Attends primary schools in Tokyo.

1876 – Returns home with stepmother after divorce from her husband, but retains the name of Shiobara.

1878–1884 – Attends secondary schools in Tokyo; studies Chinese classics and English.

1881 – Mother dies.

1883 – Attends prep school, Kōtō Gijuku.

1884–1890 – Attends the First Higher School, majoring in English.

1888 – Regains the name of Natsume.

1889 – For the first time uses the pen name Sōseki.

1890–1893 – Attends the Tokyo Imperial University, majoring in English literature.

1892 – Joins the editorial staff of *Tetsugaku Zasshi*. Writes on Laotzu and Whitman.

1893 – Gains his BA from Tokyo Imperial University; enters the Graduate School of the University; appointed a lecturer of the Tokyo Higher Normal School. Reads a paper on the concept of nature in English poetry.

1894–1895 – Sino-Japanese War.

1895 – Accepts a position with the secondary school in Matsuyama. Composes *haiku* poetry.

1896 – Marries Nakane Kyoko.

1896–1900 – Teaches at the Fifth Higher School in Kumamoto.

1897 – Publishes 'On *Tristram Shandy*'.

1900–1902 – Sent to England to study English; stays in London.

1903 – Returns to Japan; appointed a lecturer at both the First Higher School and the Tokyo Imperial University.
In the latter, begins a series of lectures on English literature.

1904–1905 – Russo-Japanese War.

1905 – *I Am a Cat* begins to appear in *Hototogisu*; publishes *Tower of London*.

1906 – Holds the first Thursday gatherings at his home; declines the *Yomiuri* offer.
Publishes his first collection, *Seven Stories*, as well as *Botchan* and *Grass on the Wayside*; completes *I Am a Cat*.
Founding of the South Manchuria Railway Company (SMR).

1907 – Accepts the *Asahi* offer to serialize his work; resigns from the Tokyo Imperial University.
Publishes his second collection, *Three Stories*, and *The Poppy*, his first serial novel; delivers 'The Philosophical Foundations of Literature.'
SMR officially separates from the Japanese military.

1908 – Publishes *The Miner*, and *Sanshiro* delivers 'The Behaviour of the Creative Writer.'

1909 – Declines the gold cup for being voted the most popular contemporary artist in the *Taiyo*; journeys through Manchuria and Korea, September 2–October 17; agrees to take charge of the *Asahi* literary columns; starts second literary column.
Publishes *Spring Miscellanies*, a series of personal essays, as well as *And Then* and *Literary Theory*; *Mankan* appears, October 21–December 31.

1910 – Suffers a serious attack of ulcers at Shuzenji.
Publishes *The Gate*; begins *Recollections*.
Japanese annexation of Korea.

1911 – Declines the government's Doctor of Letters degree; on lecturing tours, suffers an attack of ulcers; treated for haemorrhoids; his fifth daughter, Hinako, dies.
Delivers 'Entertainment and Professional Activity', 'Modern Japanese Civilization', 'Content and Form', and 'Literature and Morality'.
Communist Revolution in China.

1912 – Treated again for haemorrhoids; tries watercolour painting; complains of loneliness.

1912 – Publishes *Until After the Spring Equinox*; begins *The Wayfarer*.
1913 – After an interruption, completes *The Wayfarer*; delivers 'Imitation and Independence'.
1914 – Suffers the fourth attack of ulcers.
Publishes *Kokoro*; delivers 'My Individualism'.
Death of Emperor Meiji; end of the Meiji Era.
1915 – Journeys to Kyoto, where he suffers another attack of ulcers.
Publishes *Behind the Glass Door*.
1916 – Treated for diabetes; following his last attack of ulcers, dies December 9; buried in Zoshigaya Cemetery, Tokyo.
Last (and uncompleted) novel *Light and Darkness* published.

Index

INDEX